ON RELIGION

COLLEGE TRANSLATIONS

FRIEDRICH SCHLEIERMACHER

ON RELIGION

Speeches to Its Cultured Despisers

Translated by JOHN OMAN

Abridged, with an Introduction, by
E. GRAHAM WARING
Chairman, Departments of Religion and Philosophy
LAWRENCE COLLEGE

FREDERICK UNGAR PUBLISHING CO.
NEW YORK

Translated from the German
REDEN ÜBER DIE RELIGION

INTRODUCTION

LIKE MANY historically influential books, Schleiermacher's *On Religion* has been variously interpreted. It has been blessed as freeing the religious quest from the burden of dogmatism, and cursed as dissolving the objective truth of the Christian revelation into the vapors of subjective mysticism. It has been recognized as the greatest expression of the Romantic interpretation of religion, and, together with his later magnum opus, *The Christian Faith*, as the beginning of Protestant liberalism. Since both Romanticism and liberalism have had their critics as well as adherents, such judgments will be variously evaluated. Schleiermacher has been made responsible for every good thing which has taken place in the interpretation of religion in the West in the last one hundred and fifty years; he has also been blamed for every wrong-turning and dead end pursued in that period.

For the last thirty years in Protestant thought the tendency has been to treat Schleiermacher as the "villain" of the story of modern Christian thought. Today there are signs that historical investigation of his true role may suggest a more balanced verdict. An examination of his place in the philosophical and theological traditions suggests rather different meanings than either advocates or critics have necessarily assumed.

Schleiermacher's aim in *On Religion* can be understood only in the light of the currents of thought of his time, and, to some extent at least, only in relation to his own experience. During the eighteenth century the reaction to the increasingly sterile formulas of Protestant orthodoxy had taken among the learned two forms: vigorous rejection of religion, or the development of "natural religion." One can see a certain coherence in the religious concepts of the "natural religion" movement, despite Schleiermacher's remarks about its vagueness. In its simplest forms, it represented both a revulsion of feeling against religious disputes that had provoked years of bloodshed, and a mental outlook which assumed that only that which is universal and comprehensible to any "reasonable" being can be truly significant. Both kinds of motivation rejected the minutiae of religious disputation, and pointed to such apparently "universal" and "simple" ideas as those of a Supreme Being, immortality, and future rewards and punishments as the core of "natural religion"—reasonable religion unsullied by intellectual aridity and priestly manipulation. This simple essence of religion is also the essence of Christianity; thus Christianity is, to use the title of a popular English work outlining this view, as old as creation.

Of course, no existing religion is to be equated with natural religion, but the advocates of the latter were little troubled by this fact. The "positive" religions were regarded as representing what happens to the core of religion in history; this strain of unhistorical "primitivism" may be seen in other areas of thought during the Enlightenment. Indeed, the advocates of natural religion could point with distaste to phenomena in their own times that illustrated the degradation of pure religion—the emotionalism of Moravianism and Wesleyanism, to take but two examples.

The idea of God as conceived by the exponents of natural religion was regarded as a rational idea; His existence could be demonstrated by rational argument. Classic proofs were reformulated, based upon the view of the universe as itself coherent, orderly, and eminently rational. Evidences of purpose (in terms of the criteria of human reason) were elevated into demonstrations of the existence of a law-abiding Deity. Further, the very impressiveness of the machinelike regularity of the universe was used as an argument for a Divine Cause as its origin.

The works of David Hume and Immanuel Kant represent a sweeping critique of not only the general philosophical framework of natural religion, but of its theological concepts as well. Hume's *Dialogues Concerning Natural Religion* employ rigorous logic and biting sarcasm to demonstrate the shakiness of the "proofs," both as logical arguments and as the only possible reading of the evidence. Kant, by divorcing the realm of religion and morals from that of scientific investigation, sought to lay a new ground for religion's importance in relation to the moral will; but this end was accomplished only at the cost of denying that religious concepts added in any sense to the fund of knowledge about the world.

The advocates of natural religion assumed that religion is essentially a kind of knowledge; their critics tended to accept the assumption for their own purposes. Both alike thereby show themselves the heirs of the intellectualism of Protestant orthodoxy. But the turning point was reached in Kant's revaluation of the concept of reason itself. Schleiermacher's importance in this respect came from his protest that doctrine is but a small part—often a dead part—of the whole of religion. A rigorous thinker himself, he was concerned to show that thought is not the heart of religion.

A new wind was blowing in Germany which was to challenge many of the fundamental assumptions of the Age of Enlightenment, and not least that of the primacy of reason in religion. Romanticism is a notoriously ambiguous term, but its meaning in relation to the movement of thought in Germany in the last part of the eighteenth and early part of the nineteenth centuries is both proper and reasonably precise. In place of the uniformity which had been related to universality as an ideal, the Romantic movement stressed diversity. Professor Lovejoy has demonstrated the intellectual rootage of this Romantic outlook in terms of the ancient principle of the plenitude of being. This principle sees the power of being realizing itself in a continuum of existence. Every existent expresses in its uniqueness one small aspect of the plenitude of being. This general principle the Romantic movement articulates in varying ways in ethics, in esthetics, and in religion.

Schleiermacher uses the concept of individuality as one form of this general principle. Each person—but also each group, each nation, and each religion—can express a unique and precious focus of meaning, capable of reaching reality only in this particular place and manner. The whole universe would be poorer if this specific insight or relation were not fulfilled.

From this general idea to a view of toleration in religion and in ethics is but a short step.

Schleiermacher's emphasis upon feeling is intimately related to this principle as well as to other facets of the Romantic movement. It is in feeling that the richness of diversity becomes apparent. Uniformity and universality are ideals when the abstractions of reason are most highly valued; feeling alone, in terms of the faculty psychology of the time, is capable of being the locus of the immediate awareness of the infinitely rich diversity of being.

In the first edition of *On Religion*, Schleiermacher links "feeling" and "intuition," thereby guarding himself against later interpretations which emphasized only the subjective element in his thought. It may be doubted, however, whether the omission of "intuition" from the later editions represented any increased emphasis upon the subjective. Religion arises, he insists, in that encounter of the individual with his world which precedes the conceptualization (and hence the division into subject and object) involved in rational knowledge. "Feeling" may not be the best of concepts to designate such awareness; it clearly does not emphasize the notion of response to that which is other than the one feeling. And yet this element is not absent. Nor is this grounding of encounter with God in such a prerational awareness by any means a new departure; as Tillich has suggested, it has its roots in the Augustinian-Franciscan tradition.

This tradition of what may be loosely termed Christian mysticism was mediated to Schleiermacher by his early Moravian background. Born in 1768, Friedrich Schleiermacher became in his teens a student in

Moravian schools. He found himself surrounded by the warm emotionalism of a group which emphasized personal experience in matters of religion. Though Schleiermacher found himself unable to remain at home in the intellectual patterns of Moravianism, he always cherished this experience-centeredness. Years later he spoke of his indebtedness:

> It was here that I awoke for the first time to the consciousness of the relation of man to a higher world. . . . Here it was that that mystic tendency developed itself, which has been of so much importance to me, and has supported and carried me through all the storms of scepticism. Then it was only germinating; now it has attained its full development, and I may say that after all I have passed through, I have become a Moravian again, only of a higher order.[1]

The present translation of *On Religion,* by using the term "piety" to designate the central religious experience in its relation to personality, suggests the debt Schleiermacher owed to Moravian pietism. In his usage, of course, the term means more than the classic pietist would emphasize.

In 1796, Schleiermacher went to Berlin, and his acquaintance with the brilliant Romantic circle began. It was at the urging of his friends—especially Friedrich Schlegel—that *On Religion* was first conceived. The Romantic circle represents in general the "cultured despisers" to whom the speeches are addressed.

In Schleiermacher's later career, his early ideas, as expressed in *On Religion* (1799) and its ethical companion, the *Soliloquies* (1800), received consider-

[1] From a letter; quoted in Richard B. Brandt, *The Philosophy of Schleiermacher* (New York: Harper, 1941), p. 22.

able revision. *On Religion* went through four editions, with marked changes of terminology in the second edition (1806) and the addition of extensive "explanatory notes" in the third edition (1821). The changes generally parallel the modifications in his own activities. In 1804 he became a theological teacher at Halle; in 1810 he joined the theological faculty of the new University in Berlin. In Berlin, too, he served as preacher at the Holy Trinity Church. These theological and homiletic labors caused him to examine in greater detail and with more systematic attention the issues of the definition of Christianity. The "explanatory notes" of the third edition seek to relate the thought of the young Romantic and that of the mature theologian, to rationalize *On Religion* in terms of *The Christian Faith* (1821-1822). In matters of detail this attempt is largely unsuccessful. These notes have been omitted from this edition chiefly because they throw little light upon the meaning of *On Religion*, though much on the changes in intellectual atmosphere.

It is in the broad outlines of method and emphasis that the later Schleiermacher depends upon his earlier work. The program implied in *On Religion* for the proper study of religion is broadly executed in *The Christian Faith* in relation to Christianity; doctrines are traced to and interpreted by their relation to experience. Religion as "feeling of the infinite in the finite" becomes "feeling of absolute dependence." The same problems of objective reference exist in both works. But beyond such broad relations it is perhaps not fruitful for anyone but the specialist to seek correspondence.

On Religion marks the rise of much that is distinctive in liberal Protestant thought in the succeeding period. The emphasis upon the psychological features of religion, for example, must be seen in relation to the later development of the study of the psychology of religion. Indeed, the careful empirical study of religions owes much to *On Religion*, though later developments have invalidated much of Schleiermacher's view about the pattern of the growth of religions. At the same time, one must recognize that the heritage of *On Religion* has not been wholly of uniform value. Thus, such incautious ventures as the popular attempts to present analyses of the "inner consciousness of Jesus" owe much to Schleiermacher's approach. And no one can doubt that a kind of undiscriminating relativistic "tolerantism" is also a part of its total effect.

Schleiermacher loved that in religion which was alive, and sought at once to show his "despising" friends that it was not alien to their experience of culture, and to found it in human nature in such a way as to give it independent status. The equal standing of science, morals, and religion—for the protection of each from improper incursions by the others—was his goal. His love for religion, however, did not lead him to accept any absolutization of it; indeed, he interprets Christianity as a witness against any absolutizing of the relative in a fashion quite relevant to the present scene of religious discussion.

It is here that the student of *On Religion* will find the most difficult complex of questions confronting him. A host of questions arise, centering around the matters of relativism, the awareness of evil, the relation of the individual to his social and temporal context, the scope of religious language, the forms of the religious imagination, etc. The concrete issues which Schleiermacher debates—for example, the conception of the impersonal divine—must usually be related to this more general complex of problems if their full bearing is to be appreciated.

Little has been said here about Schleiermacher's intellectual antecedents. Scholars have devoted much attention to his use of Plato, Spinoza, and Leibniz, as well as the immediate German predecessors, Kant, Jacobi, Hamann, etc. Such matters are of major import to the historian of ideas, but *On Religion* can be read with profit apart from such questions. For the work represents an honest attempt to come to terms with the difficulties posed for the religious mind by the bankruptcy of a traditional form of doctrine, and to find a new way to comprehend and express the basic element in what is experienced as supremely meaningful. It is one signpost along the never-ending road of man's effort to seek a richer and more comprehensive awareness of life's significance.

The present edition uses unchanged Oman's translation (1893) of the third German edition. It was felt that any tampering with it would demand an entirely new translation. This edition represents about 60 per cent of the original text. The omissions are for the most part of two sorts: digressions, and references to the period of composition which are relatively meaningless to the nonspecialist today. All omissions have been indicated in the customary manner (. . .).

A word should be said about the matter of transitions. Schleiermacher was not a literary master. His transitions are frequently awkward, the connection of ideas often being hidden. Some of these infelicities occur at places where omissions have been made, but the omissions do not necessarily cause them.

The most valuable literature on Schleiermacher is generally available only in German. The following, however, may prove somewhat useful to the student who wishes to go further:

The Soliloquies and *The Christian Faith* (available in translation).

Brandt, Richard B., *The Philosophy of Schleiermacher*.

Lovejoy, A. O. *The Great Chain of Being*, ch. 10, and numerous essays on Romanticism included in or cited in *Essays in the History of Ideas*.

Mackintosh, H. R., *Types of Modern Theology*, chs. 1–3.

Moore, E. C., *An Outline of the History of Christian Thought Since Kant*, ch. 3.

Otto, Rudolf, *The Idea of the Holy*.

Pfleiderer, Otto, *The Development of Theology in Germany since Kant*, Bk. 1, ch. 3.

Selbie, W. B., *Schleiermacher*.

Storrs, V. F., *The Development of English Theology in the Nineteenth Century*, ch. 13.

Tillich, Paul, "The Present Theological Situation in the Light of the Continental European Development," *Theology Today*, VI, 3 (Oct., 1949), pp. 299–310.

Walzel, Oskar, *German Romanticism*, ch. 3.

PRINCIPAL DATES FOR SCHLEIERMACHER

1768   Born in Breslau (November 21).

1783   First sent to Moravian school.

1787–89   Study at Halle.

1790–93   Tutor in family of Count Dohna of Schlobitten.

1796   Chaplain of Charité Institute, Berlin.

1799   *Reden über die Religion an die Gebildeten unter ihren Verächtern (On Religion)*.

1800   *Monologen (Soliloquies)*.

1802   Pastor in Stolpe in Pomerania.

1804   Professor of theology and university preacher at Halle.

1804–05   Published translations of Plato.

1806   *Reden* (second edition).

1808   Appointed Reformed preacher, Dreifaltigkeitskirche, Berlin.

1810   Professor of theology, Berlin.

1811   *Kurze Darstellung des theologischen Studiums*.

1821–22   *Der christliche Glaube nach den Grundsätzen der evangelischen Kirche in Zusammenhang dargestellt (The Christian Faith)*.

1821   *Reden* (third edition).

1830   *Der christliche Glaube* (second edition).

1831   *Reden* (fourth edition).

1834   Death (February 12).

FIRST SPEECH

Defense

IT MAY BE an unexpected and even a marvelous undertaking, that any one should still venture to demand from the very class that have raised themselves above the vulgar, and are saturated with the wisdom of the centuries, attention for a subject so entirely neglected by them. And I confess that I am aware of nothing that promises any easy success, whether it be in winning for my efforts your approval, or in the more difficult and more desirable task of instilling into you my thought and inspiring you for my subject. From of old faith has not been every man's affair. At all times but few have discerned religion itself, while millions, in various ways, have been satisfied to juggle with its trappings. Now especially the life of cultivated people is far from anything that might have even a resemblance to religion. Just as little, I know, do you worship the Deity in sacred retirement, as you visit the forsaken temples. In your ornamented dwellings, the only sacred things to be met with are the sage maxims of our wise men, and the splendid compositions of our poets. Suavity and sociability, art and science have so fully taken possession of your minds, that no room remains for the eternal and holy Being that lies beyond the world. I know how well you have succeeded in making your earthly life so rich and varied, that you no longer stand in need of an eternity. Having made a universe for yourselves, you are above the need of thinking of the Universe that made you. You are agreed, I know, that nothing new, nothing convincing can any more be said on this matter, which on every side by sages and seers, and I might add by scoffers and priests, has been abundantly discussed. To priests, least of all, are you inclined to listen. They have long been outcasts for you, and are declared unworthy of your trust, because they like best to lodge in the battered ruins of their sanctuary and cannot, even there, live without disfiguring and destroying it still more. All this I know, and yet, divinely swayed by an irresistible necessity within me, I feel myself compelled to speak, and cannot take back my invitation that you and none else should listen to me.

Might I ask one question? On every subject, however small and unimportant, you would most willingly be taught by those who have devoted to it their lives and their powers. In your desire for knowledge you do not avoid the cottages of the peasant or the workshops of the humble artisans. How then does it come about that, in matters of religion alone, you hold everything the more dubious when it comes from those who are experts, not only according to their own profession, but by recognition from the state, and from the people? Or can you perhaps, strangely enough, show that they are not more experienced, but maintain and cry up anything rather than religion? Scarcely, my good sirs! Not setting much store on a judgment so baseless I confess, as is right, that I also am a member of this order. I venture, though I run the risk, if you do not give me an attentive hearing, of being reckoned among the great crowd from which you admit so few exceptions. . . .

As a man I speak to you of the sacred secrets of mankind according to my views—of what was in me as with youthful enthusiasm I sought the unknown, of what since then I have thought and experienced, of the innermost springs of my being which shall for ever remain for me the highest, however I be moved by the changes of time and mankind. I do not speak from any reasoned resolve, nor from hope, nor from fear. Nor is it done from any caprice or accident. Rather it is the pure necessity of my nature; it is a divine call; it is that which determines my position in the world and makes me what I am. Wherefore, even if it were neither fitting nor prudent to speak of religion, there is something which compels me and represses with its heavenly power all those small considerations.

You know how the Deity, by an immutable law, has compelled Himself to divide His great work even to infinity. Each definite thing can only be made up by melting together two opposite activities. Each of His eternal thoughts can only be actualized in two hostile yet twin forms, one of which cannot exist except by means of the other. The whole corporeal world, insight into which is the highest aim of your researches, appears to the best instructed and most contemplative among you, simply a never-ending play of opposing forces. Each life is merely the uninterrupted manifestation of a perpetually renewed gain and loss, as each thing has its determinate existence by uniting and holding fast in a special way the opposing forces of Nature.

Wherefore the spirit also, in so far as it manifests itself in a finite life, must be subject to the same law. The human soul, as is shown both by its passing actions and its inward characteristics, has its existence chiefly in two opposing impulses. Following the one impulse, it strives to establish itself as an individual. For increase, no less than sustenance, it draws what surrounds it to itself, weaving it into its life, and absorbing it into its own being. The other impulse, again, is the dread fear to stand alone over against the Whole, the longing to surrender oneself and be absorbed in a greater, to be taken hold of and determined. All you feel and do that bears on your separate existence, all you are accustomed to call enjoyment or possession works for the first object. The other is wrought for when you are not directed towards the individual life, but seek and retain for yourselves what is the same in all and for all the same existence, that in which, therefore, you acknowledge in your thinking and acting, law and order, necessity and connection, right and fitness. Just as no material thing can exist by only one of the forces of corporeal nature, every soul shares in the two original tendencies of spiritual nature. At the extremes one impulse may preponderate almost to the exclusion of the other, but the perfection of the living world consists in this, that between these opposite ends all combinations are actually present in humanity.

And not only so, but a common band of consciousness embraces them all, so that though the man cannot be other than he is, he knows every other person as clearly as himself, and comprehends perfectly every single manifestation of humanity. Persons, however, at the extremes of this great series, are furthest removed from such a knowledge of the whole. The endeavor to appropriate, too little influenced by the opposite endeavor, takes the form of insatiable sensuality that is mindful only of its individual life, and endeavors only in an earthly way to incorporate into it more and more material and to keep itself active and strong. Swinging eternally between desire and enjoyment, such persons never get beyond consciousness of the individual, and being ever busy with mere self-regarding concerns, they are neither able to feel nor know the common, the whole being and nature of humanity. To persons, on the other hand, too forcibly seized by the opposite impulse, who, from defective power of grasp, are incapable of acquiring any characteristic, definite culture, the true life of the world must just as much remain hidden. It is not granted them to penetrate with plastic mind and to fashion something of their own, but their activity dissipates itself in a futile game with empty notions. They never make a living study of anything, but devote their whole zeal to abstract precepts that degrade everything to means, and leave nothing to be an end. They consume themselves in mistaken hate against everything that comes before them with prosperous force. How are these extremes to be brought together, and the long series be made into a closed ring, the symbol of eternity and completeness?

Persons in whom both tendencies are toned down to an unattractive equilibrium are not rare, but, in truth, they stand lower than either. For this frequent phenomenon which so many value highly, we are not indebted to a living union of both impulses, but both are distorted and smoothed away to a dull mediocrity in which no excess appears, because all fresh life is wanting. This is the position to which a false discretion seeks to bring the younger generation. But were the extremes avoided in no other way, all men would have departed from the right life and from contemplation of the truth, the higher spirit would have vanished from the world, and the will of the Deity been entirely frustrated. Elements so separated or so reduced to equilibrium would disclose little even to men of deep insight, and, for a common eye that has no power of insight to give life to the scattered bones, a world so peopled would be only a mock mirror that neither reflects their own forms nor allows them to see behind it.

Wherefore the Deity at all times sends some here and there, who in a fruitful manner are imbued with both impulses, either as a direct gift from above, or as the result of a severe and complete self-training. They are equipped with wonderful gifts, their way is made even by an almighty indwelling word. They are interpreters of the Deity and His works, and reconcilers of things that otherwise would be eternally divided. I mean, in particular, those who unite those opposing activities, by imprinting in their lives a characteristic form upon just that common nature of spirit, the shadow of which only appears to most in empty notions, as an image upon mist. They seek order and connection, right and fitness, and they find just because they do not lose themselves. Their impulse is not sighed out in inaudible wishes, but works in them as creative power. For this power they create and acquire, and not for that degraded animal sensuality. They do not devour destructively, but, creatively recasting, they breathe into life and life's tools a higher spirit, ordering and fashioning a world that bears the impress of their mind. Earthly things they wisely control, showing themselves lawgivers and inventors, heroes and compellers of nature, or, in narrower circles, as good fairies they create and diffuse in quiet a nobler happiness. By their very existence they prove themselves ambassadors of God, and mediators between limited man and infinite humanity. To them the captive under the power of empty notions may look, to perceive in their works the right object of his own incomprehensible requirements, and in their persons the material hitherto despised, with which he ought to deal. They interpret to him the misunderstood voice of God, and reconcile him to the earth and to his place thereon. Far more the earthly and sensual require such mediators from whom to learn how much of the highest nature of humanity is wanting to their own works and ways. They stand in need of such a person to oppose to their base animal enjoyment another enjoyment, the object of which is not this thing or that, but the One in All, and All in One, an object that knows no other bounds but the world, that the spirit has learned to comprehend. He is needed to show to their anxious, restless self-love, another self-love whereby man in this earthly life and along with it loves the highest and the eternal, and to their restless passionate greed a quiet and sure possession.

Acknowledge, then, with me, what a priceless gift the appearance of such a person must be when the higher feeling has risen to inspiration, and can no longer be kept silent, when every pulse-beat of his spiritual life takes communicable form in word or figure, so that, despite his indifference to the presence of others, he almost unwillingly becomes for others the master of some divine art. This is the true priest of the highest, for he brings it nearer those who are only accustomed to lay hold of the finite and the trivial. The heavenly and eternal he exhibits as an object of enjoyment and agreement, as the sole exhaustless source of the things toward which their whole endeavor is directed. In this way he strives to awaken the slumbering germ of a better humanity, to kindle love for higher things, to change the common life into a nobler, to reconcile the children of earth with the Heaven that hears them, and to counterbalance the deep attachment of the age to the baser side. This is the higher priesthood that announces the inner meaning of all spiritual secrets, and speaks from the kingdom of God. It is the source of all visions and prophecies, of all the sacred works of art and inspired speeches that are scattered abroad, on the chance of finding some receptive heart where they may bring forth fruit. . . .

To this very power I now submit, and of this very nature is my call. Permit me to speak of myself. You know that what is spoken at the instigation of piety cannot be pride, for piety is always full of humility. Piety was the mother's womb, in whose sacred darkness my young life was nourished and was prepared for a world still sealed for it. In it my spirit breathed ere it had yet found its own place in knowledge and experience. It helped me as I began to sift the faith of my fathers and to cleanse thought and feeling from the rubbish of antiquity. When the God and the immortality of my childhood vanished from my doubting eyes it remained to me. Without design of mine it guided me into active life. It showed me how, with my endowments and defects, I should keep myself holy in an undivided existence, and through it alone I have learnt friendship and love. In respect of other human excellences, before your judgment seat, ye wise and understanding of the people, I know it is small proof of possession to be able to speak of their value. They can be known from description, from observation of others, or, as all virtues are known, from the ancient and general traditions of their nature. But religion is of such a sort and is so rare, that whoever utters anything of it, must necessarily have had it, for nowhere could he have heard it. Of all that I praise, all that I feel to be the true work of religion, you will find little even in the sacred books. To the man who has not himself experienced it, it would only be an annoyance and a folly. . . .

Let us then, I pray you, examine whence exactly religion has its rise. Is it from some clear intuition, or from some vague thought? Is it from the different kinds and sects of religion found in history, or from some general idea which you have perhaps conceived arbitrarily? Some doubtless will profess the latter view. But here as in other things the ready judgment may be without ground, the matter being superficially considered and no trouble being taken to gain an accurate knowledge. Your general idea turns on fear of an eternal being, or, broadly, respect for his influence on the occurrences of this life called by you providence, on expectation of a future life after this one, called by you immortality. These two conceptions which you have rejected, are, you consider, in one way or another, the hinges of all religion. But say, my dear sirs, how you have found this; for there are two points of view from which everything taking place in man or proceeding from him may be regarded. Considered from the center outwards, that is according to its inner quality, it is an expression of human nature, based in one of its necessary modes of acting or impulses or whatever else you like to call it, for I will not now quarrel with your technical language. On the contrary, regarded from the outside, according to the definite attitude and form it assumes in particular cases, it is a product of time and history. From what side have you considered religion that great spiritual phenomenon, that you have reached the idea that everything called by this name has a common content? You can hardly affirm that it is by regarding it from within. If so, my good sirs, you would have to admit that these thoughts are at least in some way based in human nature. And should you say that as now found they have sprung only from misinterpretations or false references of a necessary human aim, it would become you to seek in it the true and eternal, and to unite your efforts to ours to free human nature from the injustice which it always suffers when aught in it is misunderstood or misdirected. . . .

But you will probably say that your idea of the content of religion is from the other view of this spiritual phenomenon. You start with the outside, with the opinions, dogmas and usages, in which every religion is presented. They always return to providence and immortality. For these externals you have sought an inward and original source in vain. Wherefore religion generally can be nothing but an empty pretense which, like a murky and oppressive atmosphere, has enshrouded part of the truth. Doubtless this is your genuine opinion. But if you really consider these two points the sum of religion in all the forms in which it has appeared in history, permit me to ask whether you have rightly observed all these phenomena and have rightly comprehended their common content? If your idea has had its rise in this way you must justify it by instances. If anyone says it is wrong and beside the mark, and if he point out something else in religion not hollow, but having a kernel of excellent quality and extraction, you must first hear and judge before you venture further to despise. Do not grudge, therefore, to listen to what I shall say to those who, from first to last, have more accurately and laboriously adhered to observation of particulars.

You are doubtless acquainted with the histories of human follies, and have reviewed the various structures of religious doctrine from the senseless fables of wanton peoples to the most refined Deism, from the rude superstition of human sacrifice to the ill-put-together fragments of metaphysics and ethics now called purified Christianity, and you have found them all without rhyme or reason. I am far from wishing to contradict you. Rather, if you really mean that the most cultured religious system is no better than the rudest, if you only perceive that the divine cannot lie in a series that ends on both sides in something ordinary and despicable, I will gladly spare you the trouble of estimating further all that lies between. Possibly they may all appear to you transitions and stages towards the final form. Out of the hand of its age each comes better polished and carved, till at length art has grown equal to that perfect plaything with which our century has presented history. But this consummation of doctrines and systems is often anything rather than consummation of religion. Nay, not infrequently, the progress of the one has not the smallest connection with the other. I cannot speak of it without indignation. All who have a regard for what issues from within the mind, and who are in earnest that every side of man be trained and exhibited, must bewail how the high and glorious is often turned from its destination and robbed of its freedom in order to be held in despicable bondage by the scholastic spirit of a barbarian and cold time. What are all these systems, considered in themselves, but the handiwork of the calculating understanding, wherein only by mutual limitation each part holds its place? What else can they be, these systems of theology, these theories of the origin and the end of the world, these analyses of the nature of an incomprehensible Being, wherein everything runs to cold argufying, and the highest can be treated in the tone of a common controversy? And this is certainly —let me appeal to your own feeling—not the character of religion.

If you have only given attention to these dogmas and opinions, therefore, you do not yet know religion itself, and what you despise is not it. Why have you not penetrated deeper to find the kernel of this shell? I am astonished at your voluntary ignorance, ye easy-going inquirers, and at the all too quiet satisfaction with which you linger by the first thing presented to you. Why do you not regard the religious life itself, and first those pious exaltations of the mind in which all other known activities are set aside or almost suppressed, and the whole soul is dissolved in the immedi-

ate feeling of the Infinite and Eternal? In such moments the disposition you pretend to despise reveals
itself in primordial and visible form. He only who has
studied and truly known man in these emotions can
rediscover religion in those outward manifestations.
He will assuredly perceive something more in them
than you. Bound up in them all something of that
spiritual matter lies, without which they could not
have arisen. But in the hands of those who do not understand how to unbind it, let them break it up and
examine it as they may, nothing but the cold dead mass
remains.

This recommendation to seek rather in those scattered and seemingly undeveloped elements your object
that you have not yet found in the developed and the
complete to which you have hitherto been directed,
cannot surprise you who have more or less busied
yourselves with philosophy, and are acquainted with
its fortunes. With philosophy, indeed, it should be
quite otherwise. From its nature it must strive to fashion itself into the closest connection. That special
kind of knowledge is only verified and its communication assured by its completeness, and yet even here
you must commence with the scattered and incomplete. Recollect how very few of those who, in a way
of their own, have penetrated into the secrets of nature
and spirit, viewing and exhibiting their mutual relation
and inner harmony in a light of their own, have put
forth at once a system of their knowledge. In a finer, if
more fragile form, they have communicated their dis-
coveries.

On the contrary, if you regard the systems in all
schools, how often are they mere habitations and nur-

series of the dead letter. With few exceptions, the
plastic spirit of high contemplation is too fleeting and
too free for those rigid forms whereby those who
would willingly grasp and retain what is strange, believe they are best helped. Suppose that any one held
the architects of those great edifices of philosophy,
without distinction, for true philosophers! Suppose he
would learn from them the spirit of their research!
Would you not advise him thus, "See to it, friend, that
you have not lighted upon those who merely follow,
and collect, and rest satisfied with what another has
furnished: with them you will never find the spirit of
that art: to the discoverers you must go, on whom it
surely rests." To you who seek religion I must give
the same advice. It is all the more necessary, as religion
is as far removed, by its whole nature, from all that is
systematic as philosophy is naturally disposed to it.

Consider only with whom those ingenious erections originate, the mutability of which you scorn, the
bad proportions of which offend you, and the incongruity of which, with your contemptuous tendency,
almost strikes you as absurd. Have they come from the
heroes of religion? Name one among those who have
brought down any kind of new revelation to us, who
has thought it worth his while to occupy himself with
such a labor of Sisyphus, beginning with Him who
first conceived the idea of the kingdom of God, from
which, if from anything in the sphere of religion, a
system might have been produced to the new mystics
or enthusiasts, as you are accustomed to call them, in
whom, perhaps, an original beam of the inner light still
shines. You will not blame me if I do not reckon
among them the theologians of the letter, who believe

the salvation of the world and the light of wisdom are to be found in a new vesture of formulas, or a new arrangement of ingenious proofs. In isolation only the mighty thunder of their speech, announcing that the Deity is revealing Himself through them, is accustomed to be heard when the celestial feelings are unburdened, when the sacred fires must burst forth from the overcharged spirit. Idea and word are simply the necessary and inseparable outcome of the heart, only to be understood by it and along with it. Doctrine is only united to doctrine occasionally to remove misunderstanding or expose unreality.

From many such combinations those systems were gradually compacted. Wherefore, you must not rest satisfied with the repeated oft-broken echo of that original sound. You must transport yourselves into the interior of a pious soul and seek to understand its inspiration. In the very act, you must understand the production of light and heat in a soul surrendered to the Universe. Otherwise you learn nothing of religion, and it goes with you as with one who should too late bring fuel to the fire which the steel has struck from the flint, who finds only a cold, insignificant speck of coarse metal with which he can kindle nothing any more.

I ask, therefore, that you turn from everything usually reckoned religion, and fix your regard on the inward emotions and dispositions, as all utterances and acts of inspired men direct. Despite your acquirements, your culture and your prejudices, I hope for good success. . . .

Yet you need not fear that I shall betake myself in the end to that common device of representing how necessary religion is for maintaining justice and order in the world. Nor shall I remind you of an all-seeing eye, nor of the unspeakable short-sightedness of human management, nor of the narrow bounds of human power to render help. Nor shall I say how religion is a faithful friend and useful stay of morality, how, by its sacred feelings and glorious prospects, it makes the struggle with self and the perfecting of goodness much easier for weak man. Those who profess to be the best friends and most zealous defenders do indeed speak in this way. Which of the two is more degraded in being thus thought of together, I shall not decide, whether justice and morality which are represented as needing support, or religion which is to support them, or even whether it be not you to whom such things are said.

Though otherwise this wise counsel might be given you, how could I dare to suppose that you play with your consciences a sort of fast and loose game, and could be impelled by something you have hitherto had no cause to respect and love to something else that without it you already honor, and to which you have already devoted yourselves? Or suppose that these Speeches were merely to suggest what you should do for the sake of the people! How could you, who are called to educate others and make them like yourselves, begin by deceiving them, offering them as holy and vitally necessary what is in the highest degree indiffer-ent to yourselves, and which, in your opinion, they can again reject as soon as they have attained your level? I, at least, cannot invite you to a course of action in which I perceive the most ruinous hypocrisy to-ward the world and toward yourselves. To recom-

mend religion by such means would only increase the
contempt to which it is at present exposed. . . .

Just as little can morality be in need of religion.
A weak, tempted heart must take refuge in the thought
of a future world. But it is folly to make a distinction
between this world and the next. Religious persons at
least know only one. If the desire for happiness is
foreign to morality, later happiness can be no more
valid than earlier; if it should be quite independent of
praise, dread of the Eternal cannot be more valid than
dread of a wise man. If morality loses in splendor and
stability by every addition, how much more must it
lose from something that can never hide its foreign
extraction.

All this, however, you have heard of sufficiently
from those who defend the independence and might
of the moral law. Yet let me add, that to wish to
transport religion into another sphere that it may
serve and labor is to manifest toward it also great contempt. It is not so ambitious of conquest as to seek to
reign in a foreign kingdom. The power that is its
due, being earned afresh at every moment, satisfies it.
Everything is sacred to it, and above all everything
holding with it the same rank in human nature. But
it must render a special service; it must have an aim;
it must show itself useful! What degradation! And its
defenders should be eager for it! . . .

An imaginary praise that vanishes on closer contemplation, cannnot avail anything going about with
higher pretensions. I maintain that in all better souls
piety springs necessarily by itself; that a province of
its own in the mind belongs to it, in which it has un-

limited sway; that it is worthy to animate most profoundly the noblest and best and to be fully accepted and known by them. That is my contention, and it now behooves you to decide whether it is worth your while to hear me, before you still further strengthen yourselves in your contempt.

SECOND SPEECH

The Nature of Religion

You KNOW HOW the aged Simonides, by long and
repeated hesitation, put to silence the person who
troubled him with the question, What are the gods?
Our question, What is religion? is similar and equally
extensive, and I would fain begin with a like hesitation.
Naturally I would not mean by ultimate silence, as he
did, to leave you in perplexity. But you might attempt
something for yourselves; you might give steady and
continuous attention to the point about which we are
inquiring; you might entirely exclude other thoughts.
Do not even conjurors of common spirits demand ab-
stinence from earthly things and solemn stillness, as
a preparation, and undistracted, close attention to the
place where the apparition is to show itself? How
much more should I claim? It is a rare spirit that I am
to call forth, which can, only when long regarded
with fixed attention, be recognized as the object of
your desire. You must have that unbiased sobriety of
judgment that seizes clearly and accurately every outline. Without being misled by old memories or hin-
dered by preconceptions, you must endeavor to understand the object presented simply by itself. Even
then it may not win your love, and otherwise I cannot

19

hope for any unanimity about the meaning of religion or any recognition of its worth.

I could wish to exhibit religion in some well known form, reminding you, by feature, carriage and deportment, of what here and there at least you have seen in life. Religion, however, as I wish to show it, which is to say, in its own original, characteristic form, is not accustomed to appear openly, but is only seen in secret by those who love it. Not that this applies to religion alone. Nothing that is essentially characteristic and peculiar can be quite the same as that which openly exhibits and represents it. . . . Just as among civilized peoples, by extensive intercourse their characteristic ways of thought no longer appear unalloyed, so in the human mind there is such a complete sociableness founded, that no special faculty or capacity, however much it may be separated for observation, can ever, in separation, produce its work. Speaking broadly, one is, in operation, influenced and permeated by the ready love and support of the others. The predominating power is all you can distinguish. Wherefore every activity of the spirit is only to be understood, in so far as a man can study it in himself. . . .

Religion is for you at one time a way of thinking, a faith, a peculiar way of contemplating the world, and of combining what meets us in the world: at another, it is a way of acting, a peculiar desire and love, a special kind of conduct and character. Without this distinction of a theoretical and practical you could hardly think at all, and though both sides belong to religion, you are usually accustomed to give heed chiefly to only one at a time. Wherefore, we shall look closely at religion from both sides.

We commence with religion as a kind of activity. Activity is twofold, having to do with life and with art. You would ascribe with the poet earnestness to life and cheerfulness to art; or, in some other way, you would contrast them. Separate them you certainly will. For life, duty is the watchword. The moral law shall order it, and virtue shall show itself the ruling power in it, that the individual may be in harmony with the universal order of the world, and may nowhere encroach in a manner to disturb and confuse. This life, you consider, may appear without any discernible trace of art. Rather is it to be attained by rigid rules that have nothing to do with the free and variable precepts of art. Nay, you look upon it almost as a rule that art should be somewhat in the background, and non-essential for those who are strictest in the ordering of life. On the other hand, imagination shall inspire the artist, and genius shall completely sway him. Now imagination and genius are for you quite different from virtue and morality, being capable of existing in the largest measure along with a much more meagre moral endowment. Nay you are inclined, because the prudent power often comes into danger by reason of the fiery power, to relax for the artist somewhat of the strict demands of life.

How now does it stand with piety, in so far as you regard it as a peculiar kind of activity? Has it to do with right living? Is it something good and praiseworthy, yet different from morality, for you will not hold them to be identical? But in that case morality does not exhaust the sphere which it should govern. Another power works alongside of it, and has both right and might to continue working. Or will you perhaps betake yourselves to the position that piety is a virtue, and religion a duty or section of duties? Is religion incorporated into morality and subordinated to it, as a part to the whole? Is it, as some suppose, special duties toward God, and therefore a part of all morality which is the performance of all duties? But, if I have rightly appreciated or accurately reproduced what you say, you do not think so. You rather seem to say that the pious person has something entirely peculiar, both in his doing and leaving undone, and that morality can be quite moral without therefore being pious.

And how are religion and art related? They can hardly be quite alien, because, from of old, what is greatest in art has had a religious character. When, therefore, you speak of an artist as pious, do you still grant him that relaxation of the strict demands of virtue? Rather he is then subjected, like every other person. But then to make the cases parallel, you must secure that those who devote themselves to life do not remain quite without art. Perhaps this combination gives its peculiar form to religion. With your view, there seems no other possible issue.

Religion then, as a kind of activity, is a mixture of elements that oppose and neutralize each other. Pray, is not this rather the utterance of your dislike than your conviction? Such an accidental shaking together, leaving both elements unaltered, does not, even though the most accurate equality be attained, make something specific. But suppose it is otherwise, suppose piety is something which truly fuses both, then it cannot be formed simply by bringing the two together, but must be an original unity. Take care, however, I warn you, that you do not make such an admission. Were it the case, morality and genius apart would be only fragments of the ruin of religion, or its corpse when it is dead. Religion were then higher than both, the true divine life itself. But, in return for this warning, if you accept it, and discover no other solution, be so good as tell me how your opinion about religion is to be distinguished from nothing? Till then nothing remains for me but to assume that you have not yet, by examination, satisfied yourselves about this side of religion. Perhaps we shall have better fortune with the other side—what is known as the way of thinking, or faith.

You will, I believe, grant that your knowledge, however many-sided it may appear, falls, as a whole, into two contrasted sciences. How you shall subdivide and name belongs to the controversies of your schools, with which at present I am not concerned. Do not, therefore, be too critical about my terminology, even though it come from various quarters. Let us call the one division physics or metaphysics, applying both names indifferently, or indicating sections of the same thing. Let the other be ethics or the doctrine of duties or practical philosophy. At least we are agreed about the distinction meant. The former describes the nature of things, or if that seems too much, how man conceives and must conceive of things and of the world as the sum of things. The latter science, on the contrary, teaches what man should be for the world, and what he should do in it. Now, in so far as religion is a way of thinking of something and a knowledge about something, has it not the same object as these sciences? What does faith know about except the relation of man to God and to the world—God's purpose in making him, and the world's power to help or hinder him? Again it distinguishes in its own fashion a good action from a bad. Is then religion identical with natural science and ethics? You would not agree, you would never grant that our faith is as surely founded, or stands on the same level of certainty as your scientific knowledge! Your accusation against it is just that it does not know how to distinguish between the demonstrable and the probable. Similarly, you do not forget to remark diligently that very marvelous injunctions both to do and leave undone have issued from religion. You may be quite right; only do not forget that it has been the same with that which you call science. In both spheres you believe you have made improvements and are better than your fathers.

What then, are we to say that religion is? As before, that it is a mixture—mingled theoretical and practical knowledge? But this is even less permissible, particularly if, as appears, each of these two branches of knowledge has its own characteristic mode of procedure. Such a mixture of elements that would either counteract or separate, could only be made most arbitrarily. The utmost gain to be looked for would be to furnish us with another method for putting known results into shape for beginners, and for stimulating them to a further study. But if that be so, why do you strive against religion? You might, so long as beginners are to be found, leave it in peace and security. If we presumed to subject you, you might smile at our folly, but, knowing for certain that you have left it far behind, and that it is only prepared for us by you wiser people, you would be wrong in losing a serious word on the matter. But it is not so, I think. Unless I am quite mistaken, you have long been laboring to provide the mass of the people with just such an epitome of your knowledge. The name is of no consequence, whether it be "religion" or "enlightenment" or aught else. But there is something different which must first be expelled, or, at least, excluded. This something it is that you call belief, and it is the object of your hostility, and not an article you would desire to extend.

Wherefore, my friends, belief must be something different from a mixture of opinions about God and the world, and of precepts for one life or for two. Piety cannot be an instinct craving for a mess of metaphysical and ethical crumbs. If it were, you would scarcely oppose it. It would not occur to you to speak of religion as different from your knowledge, however much it might be distant. The strife of the cultured and learned with the pious would simply be the strife of depth and thoroughness with superficiality; it would be the strife of the master with pupils who are to emancipate themselves in due time. . . .

Let us be honest with one another. As we recently agreed, you have no liking for religion. But, in carrying on an honorable war which is not quite without strain, you would not wish to fight against such a shadow as that with which we have so far been battling. It must be something special that could fashion itself so peculiarly in the human heart, something thinkable, the real nature of which can so be presented as to be spoken of and argued about, and I consider it very wrong that out of things so disparate as modes of knowing and modes of acting, you patch together an untenable something, and call it religion, and then are so needlessly ceremonious with it. But you would deny that you have not gone to work with straightforwardness. Seeing I have rejected systems, commentaries and apologies, you would demand that I unfold all the original sources of religion from the beautiful fictions of the Greeks to the sacred scriptures of the Christians. Should I not find everywhere the nature of the Gods, and the will of the Gods? Is not that man everywhere accounted holy and blessed who knows the former, and does the latter?

But that is just what I have already said. Religion never appears quite pure. Its outward form is ever determined by something else. Our task first is to exhibit its true nature, and not to assume off-hand, as you seem to do, that the outward form and the true nature are the same. Does the material world present you with any element in its original purity as a spontaneous product of nature? Must you, therefore, as you have done in the intellectual world, take very gross things for simple? It is the one ceaseless aim of all analysis to present something really simple. So also it is in spiritual things. You can only obtain what is original by producing it, as it were, by a second, an artificial creation in yourselves, and even then it is but for the moment of its production. Pray come to an understanding on the point, for you shall be ceaselessly reminded of it. . . .

In order to make quite clear to you what is the original and characteristic possession of religion, it resigns, at once, all claims on anything that belongs either to science or morality. Whether it has been borrowed or bestowed it is now returned. What then does your science of being, your natural science, all your theoretical philosophy, in so far as it has to do with the actual world, have for its aim? To know things, I suppose, as they really are; to show the peculiar relations by which each is what it is; to determine for each its place in the Whole, and to distinguish it rightly from all else; to present the whole real world in its mutually conditioned necessity; and to exhibit the oneness of all phenomena with their eternal laws. This is truly beautiful and excellent, and I am not disposed to depreciate. Rather, if this description of mine, so slightly sketched, does not suffice, I will grant the highest and most exhaustive you are able to give.

And yet, however high you go; though you pass from the laws to the Universal Lawgiver, in whom is the unity of all things; though you allege that nature cannot be comprehended without God, I would still maintain that religion has nothing to do with this knowledge, and that, quite apart from it, its nature can be known. Quantity of knowledge is not quantity of piety. Piety can gloriously display itself, both with originality and individuality, in those to whom this kind of knowledge is not original. They may only know it as everybody does, as isolated results known in connection with other things. The pious man must, in a sense, be a wise man, but he will readily admit, even though you somewhat proudly look down upon him, that, in so far as he is pious, he does not hold his knowledge in the same way as you.

Let me interpret in clear words what most pious persons only guess at and never know how to express. Were you to set God at the apex of your science as the foundation of all knowing as well as of all knowledge, they would accord praise and honor, but it would not be their way of having and knowing God. From their way, as they would readily grant, and as is easy enough to see, knowledge and science do not proceed.

It is true that religion is essentially contemplative. You would never call anyone pious who went about in impervious stupidity, whose sense is not open for the life of the world. But this contemplation is not turned, as your knowledge of nature is, to the existence of a finite thing, combined with and opposed to another finite thing. It has not even, like your knowledge of God—if for once I might use an old expression—to do with the nature of the first cause, in itself and in its relation to every other cause and operation. The contemplation of the pious is the immediate consciousness of the universal existence of all finite things, in and through the Infinite, and of all temporal things in and through the Eternal. Religion is to seek this and find it in all that lives and moves, in all growth and change, in all doing and suffering. It is to have life and to know life in immediate feeling, only as such an existence in the Infinite and Eternal. Where this is found religion is satisfied, where it hides itself there is for her unrest and anguish, extremity and death. Wherefore it is a life in the infinite nature of the Whole, in the One and in the All, in God, having and possessing all things in God, and God in all. Yet religion is not knowledge and science, either of the world or of God. Without being knowledge, it recognizes knowledge and science. In itself it is an affection, a revelation of the Infinite in the finite, God being seen in it and it in God.

Similarly, what is the object of your ethics, of your science of action? Does it not seek to distinguish precisely each part of human doing and producing, and at the same time to combine them into a whole, according to actual relations? But the pious man confesses that, as pious, he knows nothing about it. He does, indeed, contemplate human action, but it is not the kind of contemplation from which an ethical system takes its rise. Only one thing he seeks out and detects, action from God, God's activity among men. If your ethics are right, and his piety as well, he will not, it is true, acknowledge any action as excellent which is not embraced in your system. But to know and to construct this system is your business, ye learned, not his. If you will not believe, regard the case of women. You ascribe to them religion, not only as an adornment, but you demand of them the finest feeling for distinguishing the things that excel: do you equally expect them to know your ethics as a science?

It is the same, let me say at once, with action itself. The artist fashions what is given him to fashion, by virtue of his special talent. These talents are so different that the one he possesses another lacks; unless someone, against heaven's will, would possess all. But when anyone is praised to you as pious, you are not accustomed to ask which of these gifts dwell in him by virtue of his piety. The citizen—taking the word in the sense of the ancients, not in its present meager significance—regulates, leads, and influences in virtue of his morality. But this is something different from piety. Piety has also a passive side. While morality always shows itself as manipulating, as self-controlling, piety appears as a surrender, a submission to be moved by the Whole that stands over against man. Morality depends, therefore, entirely on the consciousness of freedom, within the sphere of which all that it produces falls. Piety, on the contrary, is not at all bound to this side of life. In the opposite sphere of necessity, where there is no properly individual action, it is quite as active. Wherefore the two are different. Piety does, indeed, linger with satisfaction on every action that is from God, and every activity that reveals the Infinite in the finite, and yet it is not itself this activity. Only by keeping quite outside the range both of science and of practice can it maintain its proper sphere and character. Only when piety takes its place alongside of science and practice, as a necessary, an indispensable third, as their natural counterpart, not less in worth and splendor than either, will the common field be altogether occupied and human nature on this side complete.

But pray understand me fairly. I do not mean that one could exist without the other, that, for example, a man might have religion and be pious, and at the same time be immoral. That is impossible. But, in my opinion, it is just as impossible to be moral or scientific without being religious. But have I not said that religion can be had without science? Wherefore, I have myself begun the separation. But remember, I only said piety is not the measure of science. Just as one cannot be truly scientific without being pious, the pious man may not know at all, but he cannot know falsely. His proper nature is not of that subordinate kind, which, according to the old adage that like is only known to like, knows nothing except semblance of reality.

His nature is reality which knows reality, and where it encounters nothing it does not suppose it sees something. And what a precious jewel of science, in my view, is ignorance for those who are captive to semblance. If you have not learned it from my Speeches or discovered it for yourselves, go and learn it from your Socrates. Grant me consistency at least. With ignorance your knowledge will ever be mixed, but the true and proper opposite of knowledge is presumption of knowledge. By piety this presumption is most certainly removed, for with it piety cannot exist.

Such a separation of knowledge and piety, and of action and piety, do not accuse me of making. You are only ascribing to me, without my deserving it, your own view and the very confusion, as common as it is unavoidable, which it has been my chief endeavor to show you in the mirror of my Speech. Just because you do not acknowledge religion as the third, knowledge and action are so much apart that you can discover no unity, but believe that right knowing can be had without right acting, and *vice versa*. I hold that it is only in contemplation that there is division. There, where it is necessary, you despise it, and instead transfer it to life, as if in life itself objects could be found independent one of the other. Consequently you have no living insight into any of these activities. Each is for you a part, a fragment. Because you do not deal with life in a living way, your conception bears the stamp of perishableness, and is altogether meager. True science is complete vision; true practice is culture and art self-produced; true religion is sense and taste for the Infinite. To wish to have true science or true practice without religion, or to imagine it is possessed, is obstinate, arrogant delusion, and culpable error. It issues from the unholy sense that would rather have a show of possession by cowardly purloining than have secure possession by demanding and waiting. What can man accomplish that is worth speaking of, either in life or in art, that does not arise in his own self from the influence of this sense for the Infinite? Without it, how can anyone wish to comprehend the world scientifically, or if, in some distinct talent, the knowledge is thrust upon him, how should he wish to exercise it? What is all science, if not the existence of things in you, in your reason? what is all art and culture if not your existence in the things to which you give measure, form and order? And how can both come to life in you except in so far as there lives immediately in you the eternal unity of Reason and Nature, the universal existence of all finite things in the Infinite?

Wherefore, you will find every truly learned man devout and pious. Where you see science without religion, be sure it is transferred, learned up from another. It is sickly, if indeed it is not that empty appearance which serves necessity and is no knowledge at all. And what else do you take this deduction and weaving together of ideas to be, which neither live nor correspond to any living thing? Or in ethics, what else is this wretched uniformity that thinks it can grasp the highest human life in a single dead formula? The former arises because there is no fundamental feeling of that living nature which everywhere presents variety and individuality, and the latter because the sense fails to give infinity to the finite by determining its nature and boundaries only from the Infinite. Hence the dominion of the mere notion; hence the mechanical erections of your systems instead of an organic structure; hence the vain juggling with analytical formulas, in which, whether categorical or hypothetical, life will not be fettered. Science is not your calling, if you despise religion and fear to surrender yourself to reverence and aspiration for the primordial. Either science must become as low as your life, or it must be separated and stand alone, a division that precludes success. If man is not one with the Eternal in the unity of intuition and feeling which is immediate, he remains, in the unity of consciousness which is derived, for ever apart. . . .

But, in order that you may understand what I mean by this unity and difference of religion, science and art, we shall endeavor to descend into the inmost sanctuary of life. There, perhaps, we may find ourselves agreed. There alone you discover the original relation of intuition and feeling from which alone this identity and difference is to be understood. But I must direct you to your own selves. You must apprehend a living movement. You must know how to listen to yourselves before your own consciousness. At least you must be able to reconstruct from your consciousness your own state. What you are to notice is the rise of your consciousness and not to reflect upon something already there. Your thought can only embrace what is sundered. Wherefore as soon as you have made any given definite activity of your soul an object of communication or of con-

templation, you have already begun to separate. It
is impossible, therefore, to adduce any definite example, for, as soon as anything is an example, what I
wish to indicate is already past. Only the faintest
trace of the original unity could then be shown. Such
as it is, however, I will not despise it, as a preliminary.

Consider how you delineate an object. Is there
not both a stimulation and a determination by the
object, at one and the same time, which for one particular moment forms your existence? The more
definite your image, the more, in this way, you become the object, and the more you lose yourselves.
But just because you can trace the growing preponderance of one side over the other, both must have been
one and equal in the first, the original movement that
has escaped you. Or sunk in yourselves you find all
that you formerly regarded as a disconnected manifold
compacted now indivisibly into the one peculiar content of your being. Yet when you give heed, can
you not see as it disappears, the image of an object,
from whose influence, from whose magical contact
this definite consciousness has proceeded? The more
your own state sways you the paler and more un-
recognizable your image becomes. The greater your
emotion, the more you are absorbed in it, the more
your whole nature is concerned to retain for the
memory an imperishable trace of what is necessarily
fleeting, to carry over to what you may engage in,
its color and impress, and so unite two moments into
a duration, the less you observe the object that caused
it. But just because it grows pale and vanishes, it must
before have been nearer and clearer. Originally it must
have been one and the same with your feeling. But,

as was said, these are mere traces. Unless you will go back on the first beginning of this consciousness, you can scarcely understand them.

And suppose you cannot? Then say, weighing it quite generally and originally, what is every act of your life in itself and without distinction from other acts. What is it merely as act, as movement? Is it not the coming into being of something for itself, and at the same time in the Whole? It is an endeavor to return into the Whole, and to exist for oneself at the same time. These are the links from which the whole chain is made. Your whole life is such an existence for self in the Whole. How now are you in the Whole? By your senses. And how are you for yourselves? By the unity of your self-consciousness, which is given chiefly in the possibility of comparing the varying degrees of sensation. How both can only rise together, if both together fashion every act of life, is easy to see. You become sense and the Whole becomes object. Sense and object mingle and unite, then each returns to its place, and the object rent from sense is a perception, and you, rent from the object, are for yourselves, a feeling. It is this earlier moment I mean, which you always experience yet never experience. The phenomenon of your life is just the result of its constant departure and return. It is scarcely in time at all, so swiftly it passes; it can scarcely be described, so little does it properly exist. Would that I could hold it fast and refer to it your commonest as well as your highest activities. . . .

It is the first contact of the universal life with an individual. It fills no time and fashions nothing palpable. It is the holy wedlock of the Universe with the incarnated Reason for a creative, productive embrace. It is immediate, raised above all error and misunderstanding. You lie directly on the bosom of the infinite world. In that moment, you are its soul. Through one part of your nature you feel, as your own, all its powers and its endless life. In that moment it is your body, you pervade, as your own, its muscles and members and your thinking and forecasting set its inmost nerves in motion. In this way every living, original movement in your life is first received. Among the rest it is the source of every religious emotion. But it is not, as I said, even a moment. The incoming of existence to us, by this immediate union, at once stops as soon as it reaches consciousness. Either the intuition displays itself more vividly and clearly, like the figure of the vanishing mistress to the eyes of her lover; or feeling issues from your heart and overspreads your whole being, as the blush of shame and love over the face of the maiden. At length your consciousness is finally determined as one or other, as intuition or feeling. Then, even though you have not quite surrendered to this division and lost consciousness of your life as a unity, there remains nothing but the knowledge that they were originally one, that they issued simultaneously from the fundamental relation of your nature. Wherefore, it is in this sense true what an ancient sage has taught you, that all knowledge is recollection. It is recollection of what is outside of all time, and is therefore justly to be placed at the head of all temporal things.

And, as it is with intuition and feeling on the one hand, so it is with knowledge which includes both and with activity on the other. Through the constant play and mutual influence of these opposites, your life expands and has its place in time. Both knowledge and activity are a desire to be identified with the Universe through an object. If the power of the objects preponderates, if, as intuition or feeling, it enters and seeks to draw you into the circle of their existence, it is always a knowledge. If the pre-ponderating power is on your side, so that you give the impress and reflect yourselves in the objects, it is activity in the narrower sense, external working. Yet it is only as you are stimulated and determined that you can communicate yourselves to things. In founding or establishing anything in the world you are only giving back what that original act of fellowship has wrought in you, and similarly everything the world fashions in you must be by the same act. One must mutually stimulate the other. Only in an interchange of knowing and activity can your life consist. A peaceful existence, wherein one side did not stimulate the other, would not be your life. It would be that from which it first developed, and into which it will again disappear.

There then you have the three things about which my Speech has so far turned,—perception, feeling and activity, and you now understand what I mean when I say they are not identical and yet are inseparable. Take what belongs to each class and consider it by itself. You will find that those moments in which you exercise power over things and impress your-selves upon them, form what you call your practical, or, in the narrower sense, your moral life; again the contemplative moments, be they few or many, in which things produce themselves in you as intuition, you will doubtless call your scientific life. Now can either series alone form a human life? Would it not be death? If each activity were not stimulated and renewed by the other, would it not be self-consumed? Yet they are not identical. If you would understand your life and speak comprehensibly of it, they must be distinguished. As it stands with these two in respect of one another, it must stand with the third in respect of both. How then are you to name this third, which is the series of feeling? What life will it form? The religious as I think, and as you will not be able to deny, when you have considered it more closely.

The chief point in my Speech is now uttered. This is the peculiar sphere which I would assign to religion—the whole of it, and nothing more. . . . Your feeling is piety, in so far as it expresses, in the manner described, the being and life common to you and to the All. Your feeling is piety in so far as it is the result of the operation of God in you by means of the operation of the world upon you. This series is not made up either of perceptions or of objects of perception, either of works or operations or of different spheres of operation, but purely of sensations and the influence of all that lives and moves around, which accompanies them and conditions them. These feelings are exclusively the elements of religion, and none are excluded. There is no sensation that is not pious, except it indicate some diseased and impaired state of the life, the influence of which will not be confined to religion. Wherefore, it follows that ideas and principles are all foreign to religion. This truth we here come upon for the second time. If ideas and principles are to be anything, they must belong to knowledge which is a different department of life from religion.

Now that we have some ground beneath us, we are in a better position to inquire about the source of this confusion. May there not be some reason for this constant connection of principles and ideas with religion? In the same way is there not a cause for the connection of action with religion? Without such an inquiry it would be vain to proceed farther. The misunderstanding would be confirmed, for you would change what I say into ideas and begin seeking for principles in them. Whether you will follow my exposition, who can tell? What now is to hinder that each of the functions of life just indicated should not be an object for the others? Or does it not rather manifestly belong to their inner unity and equality that they should in this manner strive to pass over into one another? So at least it seems to me. Thus, as a feeling person, you can become an object to yourself and you can contemplate your own feeling. Nay, you can, as a feeling person, become an object for yourself to operate upon and more and more to impress your deepest nature upon. Would you now call the general description of the nature of your feelings that is the product of this contemplation a principle, and the description of each feeling, an idea, you are certainly free to do so. And if you call them religious principles and ideas, you are not in error. But do not forget that this is scientific treatment of religion, knowledge about it, and not religion itself.

Nor can the description be equal to the thing described. The feeling may dwell in many sound and strong, as for example in almost all women, without ever having been specially a matter of contemplation. Nor may you say religion is lacking, but only knowledge about religion. Furthermore, do not forget what we have already established, that this contemplation presupposes the original activity. It depends entirely upon it. If the ideas and principles are not from reflection on a man's own feeling, they must be learned by rote and utterly void. Make sure of this, that no man is pious, however perfectly he understands these principles and conceptions, however much he believes he possesses them in clearest consciousness, who cannot show that they have originated in himself and, being the outcome of his own feeling, are peculiar to himself. Do not present him to me as pious, for he is not. . . . From within, in their original, characteristic form, the emotions of piety must issue. They must be indubitably your own feelings, and not mere stale descriptions of the feelings of others, which could at best issue in a wretched imitation.

Now the religious ideas which form those systems can and ought to be nothing else than such a description, for religion cannot and will not originate in the pure impulse to know. What we feel and are conscious of in religious emotions is not the nature of things, but their operation upon us. What you may know or believe about the nature of things is far beneath the sphere of religion. The Universe is ceaselessly active and at every moment is revealing itself to us. Every form it has produced, everything to which, from the fulness of its life, it has given a separate existence, every occurrence scattered from its fertile bosom is an operation of the Universe upon us.

Now religion is to take up into our lives and to submit to be swayed by them, each of these influences and their consequent emotions, not by themselves but as a part of the Whole, not as limited and in opposition to other things, but as an exhibition of the Infinite in our life. Anything beyond this, any effort to penetrate into the nature and substance of things is no longer religion, but seeks to be a science of some sort.

On the other hand, to take what are meant as descriptions of our feelings for a science of the object, in some way the revealed product of religion, or to regard it as science and religion at the same time, necessarily leads to mysticism and vain mythology. . . . The sum total of religion is to feel that, in its highest unity, all that moves us in feeling is one; to feel that aught single and particular is only possible by means of this unity; to feel, that is to say, that our being and living is a being and living in and through God. But it is not necessary that the Deity should be presented as also one distinct object. To many this view is necessary, and to all it is welcome, yet it is always hazardous and fruitful in difficulties. It is not easy to avoid the appearance of making Him susceptible of suffering like other objects. It is only one way of characterizing God, and, from the difficulties of it, common speech will probably never rid itself. But to treat this objective conception of God just as if it were a perception, as if apart from His operation upon us through the world the existence of God before the world, and outside of the world, though for the world, were either by or in religion exhibited as science is, so far as religion is concerned, vain mythology. What is only a help for presentation is treated as a reality. It is a misunderstanding very easily made, but it is quite outside the peculiar territory of religion.

From all this you will at once perceive how the question, whether religion is a system or not, is to be treated. It admits of an entire negative, and also of a direct affirmative, in a way that perhaps you scarce expected. Religion is certainly a system, if you mean that it is formed according to an inward and necessary connection. That the religious sense of one person is moved in one way, and that of another in another is not pure accident, as if the emotions formed no whole, as if any emotions might be caused in the same individual by the same object. Whatever occurs anywhere, whether among many or few as a peculiar and distinct kind of feeling is in itself complete, and by its nature necessary. What you find as religious emotions among Turks or Indians, cannot equally appear among Christians. The essential oneness of religiousness spreads itself out in a great variety of provinces, and again, in each province it contracts itself, and the narrower and smaller the province there is necessarily more excluded as incompatible and more included as characteristic. Christianity, for example, is a whole in itself, but so is any of the divisions that may at any time have appeared in it, down to Protestantism and Catholicism in modern times. Finally, the piety of each individual, whereby he is rooted in the greater unity, is a whole by itself. It is a rounded whole, based on his peculiarity, on what you call his character, of which it forms one side. Religion thus fashions itself with endless variety, down even to the single personality.

. . . Religion is, in its individual manifestations whereby it displays itself immediately in life, from nothing farther removed than from all semblance of compulsion or limitation. In life, the necessary element is taken up, taken up into freedom. Each emotion appears as the free self-determination of this very disposition, and mirrors one passing moment of the world. . . .

True, a special type of religion is constituted by one definite kind and manner of feeling, but it is mere perversion to call it a principle, and to treat it as if the rest could be deduced from it. This distinct form of a religion is found, in the same way, in every single element of religion. Each expression of feeling bears on it immediately this peculiar impress. It cannot show itself without it, nor be comprehended without it. Everything is to be found immediately, and not proved from something else. Generals, which include particulars, combination and connection belong to another sphere, if they rest on reality, or they are merely a work of fantasy and caprice. Every man may have his own regulation and his own rubrics. What is essential can neither gain nor lose thereby. Consequently, the man who truly knows the nature of his religion, will give a very subordinate place to all apparent connection of details, and will not sacrifice the smallest for the sake of it.

By taking the opposite course, the marvelous thought has arisen of a universality of one religion, of one single form which is true, and in respect of which all others are false. Were it not that misunderstanding must be guarded against, I would say that it is only by such deducing and connecting that such a comparison as true and false, which is not peculiarly appropriate to religion, has ever been reached. It only applies where we have to do with ideas. Elsewhere the negative laws of your logic are not in place. All is immediately true in religion, for except immediately how could anything arise? But that only is immediate which has not yet passed through the stage of idea, but has grown up purely in the feeling. All that is religious is good, for it is only religious as it expresses a common higher life. But the whole circumference of religion is infinite, and is not to be comprehended under one form, but only under the sum total of all forms. It is infinite, not merely because any single religious organization has a limited horizon, and, not being able to embrace all, cannot believe that there is nothing beyond; but more particularly, because everyone is a person by himself, and is only to be moved in his own way, so that for everyone the elements of religion have most characteristic differences. Religion is infinite, not only because something new is ever being produced in time, by the endless relations both active and passive between different minds and the same limited matter; not only because the capacity for religion is never perfected, but is ever being developed anew, is ever being more beautifully reproduced, is ever entering deeper into the nature of man; but religion is infinite on all sides. As the knowledge of its eternal truth and infallibility accompanies knowledge, the consciousness of this infinity accompanies religion. It is the very feeling of religion, and must therefore accompany everyone that really has religion. He must be conscious that his religion is only part of the whole; that about the same circumstances there may be views and sentiments quite different from his, yet just as pious; and that there may be perceptions and feelings belonging to other modifications of religion, for which the sense may entirely fail him.

You see how immediately this beautiful modesty, this friendly, attractive forbearance springs from the nature of religion. How unjustly, therefore, do you reproach religion with loving persecution, with being malignant, with overturning society, and making blood flow like water. Blame those who corrupt religion, who flood it with an army of formulas and definitions, and seek to cast it into the fetters of a so-called system. What is it in religion about which men have quarrelled and made parties and kindled wars? About definitions, the practical sometimes, the theoretical always, both of which belong elsewhere. Philosophy, indeed, seeks to bring those who would know to a common knowledge. Yet even philosophy leaves room for variety, and the more readily the better it understands itself. But religion does not, even once, desire to bring those who believe and feel to one belief and one feeling. Its endeavor is to open in those who are not yet capable of religious emotions, the sense for the unity of the original source of life. But just because each seer is a new priest, a new mediator, a new organ, he flees with repugnance the bald uniformity which would again destroy this divine abundance. . . .

Seers of the Infinite have ever been quiet souls. They abide alone with themselves and the Infinite, or if they do look around them, grudge to no one who understands the mighty word his own peculiar way. By means of this wide vision, this feeling of the Infinite, they are able to look beyond their own sphere.

There is in religion such a capacity for unlimited manysidedness in judgment and in contemplation as is nowhere else to be found. I will not except even morality and philosophy, not at least so much of them as remains after religion is taken away. Let me appeal to your own experience. Does not every other object whereto man's thinking and striving are directed, draw around him a narrow circle, inside of which all that is highest for him is enclosed, and outside of which all appears common and unworthy? The man who only thinks methodically, and acts from principle and design, and will accomplish this or that in the world, unavoidably circumscribes himself, and makes everything that does not forward him an object of antipathy. Only when the free impulse of seeing, and of living is directed towards the Infinite and goes into the Infinite, is the mind set in unbounded liberty. Religion alone rescues it from the heavy fetters of opinion and desire. For it, all that is is necessary, all that can be is an indispensable image of the Infinite. In this respect, it is all worthy of preservation and contemplation, however much, in other respects, and in itself, it is to be rejected. To a pious mind religion makes everything holy, even unholiness and commonness, whether he comprehends it or does not comprehend it, whether it is embraced in his system of thought, or lies outside, whether it agrees with his peculiar mode of acting or disagrees. Religion is the natural and sworn foe of all narrowmindedness, and of all onesidedness.

These charges, therefore, do not touch religion. They rest upon the confusion between religion and that knowledge which belongs to theology. It is a knowledge, whatever be its value, and is to be always

distinguished from religion. Just as inapplicable are
the charges you have made in respect of action. . . .
In the first place, you charge religion with causing
not infrequently in the social, civil, and moral life,
improper, horrible, and even unnatural dealings. I will
not demand proof that these actions have proceeded
from pious men. I will grant it provisionally. But in
the very utterance of your accusation, you separate
religion and morality. Do you mean then that religion
is immorality, or a branch of it? Scarcely, for your
war against it would then be of quite another sort,
and you would have to make success in vanquishing
religion a test of morality. . . . Or do you only mean
that piety is different from morality, indifferent in
respect of it, and capable therefore of accidentally
becoming immoral? Piety and morality can be considered apart, and so far they are different. As I
have already admitted and asserted, the one is based
on feeling, the other on action. But how, from this
opposition do you come to make religion responsible
for action? Would it not be more correct to say that
such men were not moral enough, and had they
been, they might have been quite as pious without
harm? . . .

Religion by itself does not urge men to activity
at all. If you could imagine it implanted in man quite
alone, it would produce neither these nor any other
deeds. The man, according to what we have said,
would not act, he would only feel. Wherefore, as you
rightly complain, there have been many most religious
men in whom the proper impulses to action have been
wanting, and morality been too much in the background, who have retired from the world and have

betaken themselves in solitude to idle contemplation. Religion, when isolated and morbid, is capable of such effects, but not of cruel and horrible deeds. . . .

The whole religious life consists of two elements, that man surrender himself to the Universe and allow himself to be influenced by the side of it that is turned towards him is one part, and that he transplant this contact which is one definite feeling, within, and take it up into the inner unity of his life and being, is the other. The religious life is nothing else than the constant renewal of this proceeding. When, therefore, anyone is stirred, in a definite way, by the World, is it his piety that straightway sets him to such working and acting as bear the traces of commotion and disturb the pure connection of the moral life? Impossible. On the contrary, his piety invites him to enjoy what he has won, to absorb it, to combine it, to strip it of what is temporal and individual, that it may no more dwell in him as commotion but be quiet, pure and eternal. From this inner unity, action springs of its own accord, as a natural branch of life. As we agreed, activity is a reaction of feeling, but the sum of activity should only be a reaction of the sum of feeling, and single actions should depend on something quite different from momentary feeling. Only when each action is in its own connection and in its proper place, and not when, dependently and slavishly, it corresponds to one emotion, does it exhibit, in a free and characteristic way, the whole inner unity of the spirit.

Consequently your charge does not touch religion. And, if you are speaking of a morbid state of it, you are speaking of what is quite general and is not in any way original to religion nor specially seated in it, and from which consequently nothing is to be concluded against religion in particular. Religion is of course finite, and therefore subject to imperfections, but it must be apparent to you that, in a healthy state, man cannot be represented as acting from religion or being driven to action by religion, but piety and morality form each a series by itself and are two different functions of one and the same life. But while man does nothing from religion, he should do everything with religion. Uninterruptedly, like sacred music, the religious feelings should accompany his active life. . . .

The most general, almost preliminary truths have long delayed us. They should have been understood of themselves, but neither you, nor many who would at least wish to be counted among you, understood the relation of religion to the other branches of life. Wherefore, it was necessary to drain off at once the sources of the commonest misconceptions, that they might not afterwards retard us. This having been done to the utmost of my ability, we have now, I hope, firm ground beneath us. We have attached ourselves to that moment, which is never directly observed, but in which all the different phenomena of life fashion themselves together, as in the buds of some plants blossom and fruit are both enclosed. When, therefore, we have asked where now among all it produces is religion chiefly to be sought, we have found only one right and consistent answer. Chiefly where the living contact of man with the world fashions itself as feeling. These feelings are the beautiful and sweet scented flowers of religion, which, after the hidden activity opens, soon fall, but which the divine growth ever anew produces from the fulness of life. A climate of paradise is thus created in which no penuriousness disturbs the development, and no rude surrounding injures the tender lights and fine texture of its flowers. To this I would now conduct you, your vision having been purified and prepared.

First of all, then, follow me to outward nature, which is to many the first and only temple of the God-head. In virtue of its peculiar way of stirring the heart, it is held to be the inmost sanctuary of religion. At present, however, this outward nature, although it should be more, is little else than the outer court, for the view with which you next oppose me is utterly to be repudiated. The fear of the powers which rule in nature, which spare nothing, which threaten the life and works of man, is said to give the first feeling of the Infinite, or even to be the sole basis of religion. Surely in that case you must admit that if piety came with fear it must go with fear.

Let us then consider the matter. Manifestly the great aim of all industry spent in cultivating the earth is to destroy the dominion of the powers of nature over man, and to bring all fear of them to an end. Already a marvelous amount has been done. . . . Were fear then the ground of reverence for the powers of nature, by thus mutually destroying one another, they would gradually appear ordinary and common; for what man has controlled or attempted to control, he can measure, and what is measurable cannot stand in awful opposition to him as the Infinite. . . . If you are still capable of being filled with reverence for the great powers of nature, does it depend on your security or insecurity? . . . Is not nature protecting and sustaining quite as

much an object of adoration? Or, consider it in this
way. Does the great and infinite alone threaten man's
existence and oppose his working? Does he not also
suffer from much that is small and paltry, which, because it cannot be definitely comprehended or fashioned into something great, you call accident and the
accidental? Has this ever been made an object of
religion and been worshipped? If you have such a
small conception of the Fate of the Ancients, you must
have understood little of their poetic piety. Under this
dread Fate the sustaining powers were as much embraced as the destructive. Very different from that
slavish fear, to banish which was a credit and a virtue,
was the holy reverence for Fate, the rejection of which,
in the best and most cultured times of Antiquity, was
accounted, among better disposed persons, absolute
recklessness. Such a sacred reverence I will readily
acknowledge as the first element of religion, but the
fear you mean is not only not religion itself, it is not
even preparatory or introductory. If it should be
praised, it must be for urging men, by the desire to be
rid of it, into earthly fellowship in the state. But piety
first begins when it is put aside, for the aim of all religion is to love the World-Spirit and joyfully to regard his working, and fear is not in love.

But that joy in Nature, which so many extol, is
just as little truly religious. I almost hate to speak of
their doings when they dart off into the great, glorious
world to get for themselves little impressions: how they
inspect the delicate markings and tints of flowers, or
gaze at the magic play of colors in the glowing evening
sky, and how they admire the songs of the birds on a
beautiful countryside. They are quite full of admira-

tion and transport, and will have it that no instrument could conjure forth these sounds and no brush attain this gloss and marking. But suppose we take their course and subtilize after their fashion! What is it that they do admire? Rear the plant in a dark cellar, and, if you are successful, you can rob it of all these beauties, without in the least degree altering its nature. Suppose the vapor above us somewhat differently disposed; instead of that splendor, you would have before your eyes one unpleasant grayness, and yet what you are contemplating would be essentially the same. Once more, try to imagine how the midday sun, the glare of which you cannot endure, already appears to the inhabitants of the East the glimmering twilight. Is it not manifest, then, when they have not the same sensation, that they have gone after a mere void appearance? But they do not believe in it merely as an appearance; it is for them really true. They are in perplexity between appearance and reality, and what is so doubtful cannot be a religious stimulus, and can call forth no genuine feeling. Were they children who, without further thinking and willing, without comparison and reflection, received the light and splendor, their hearts being opened for the world by the soul of the world, so that they are stirred to pious feeling by every object; or were they sages in whose clear intuition all strife between appearance and reality is resolved, and who, therefore, undisturbed by these refinements, can again be stirred like children, their joy would be a real and pure feeling, a living impulse, a gladly communicative contact between them and the world. If you understand this better way, then you can say that this also is a necessary and indispensable element of religion. But do not present me that empty affected thing that sits so loose and is but a wretched mask for their cold, hard refinement, as an emotion of piety. In opposing religion, do not ascribe to it what does not belong to it. Do not scoff, as if man entered most easily into this sanctuary by being debased to fear of the irrational, and by vain trifling with transitory show, as if piety were easiest, and most becoming to timid, weak, sensitive souls.

The next thing to meet us in corporeal nature is its material boundlessness, the enormous masses which are scattered over illimitable space and which circulate in measureless orbits. Many hold that the exhaustion of the imagination, when we try to expand our diminished pictures of them to their natural size, is the feeling of the greatness and majesty of the Universe. This arithmetical amazement which, just on account of their ignorance, is easiest to awake in infants and ignoramuses, you are quite right in finding somewhat childish and worthless. But would those who are accustomed to take this view grant us that, when these great orbits had not yet been calculated, when half of those worlds were not discovered, nay, when it was not yet known that these shining points were worlds, piety, lacking one essential element, was necessarily poorer? . . . As long as this feeling rests on difference of mass, it is merely a feeling of personal incapacity, which is doubtless a religious feeling, but is not that glorious reverence, as exalting as it is humbling, which is the feeling of our relation to the Whole. Neither a world operation too great for an organization, nor anything beyond it from smallness, can constitute this feeling, but it must be just as strong when the operation is equal and conformable to our powers.

What moves us so wondrously is not the contrast between small and great, but the essence of greatness, the external law in virtue of which size and number in general first arose. Life alone can work on us in a characteristic way, and not what is captive to weight and in so far dead. The religious sense corresponds not to the masses in the outer world, but to their eternal laws. Rise to the height of seeing how these laws equally embrace all things, the greatest and the smallest, the world systems and the mote which floats in the air, and then say whether you are not conscious of the divine unity and the eternal immutability of the world.

By the most constant repetition, some elements in these laws cannot escape even common perception. There is the order in which all movements return in the heavens and on the earth, the recognized coming and going of all organized forces, the perpetual trust-worthiness of the rules of mechanics, and the eternal uniformity in the striving of plastic Nature. But, if it is allowable to make a comparison, this regularity gives a less great and lively religious feeling than the sense of law in all difference. Nor should this appear strange to you.

Suppose you are looking at a fragment of a great work of art. In the separate parts of this fragment you perceive beautiful outlines and situations, complete and fully to be understood without anything besides. Would not the fragment then rather appear a work by itself than a part of a greater work, and would you not judge that, if the whole was wrought throughout in this style, it must lack breadth and boldness and all that suggests a great spirit? If a loftier unity is to be suspected, along with the general tendency to order and harmony, there must be here and there situations not fully explicable. Now the world is a work of which you only see a part. Were this part perfectly ordered and complete in itself, we would be conscious of the greatness of the whole only in a limited way.

You see that the irregularity of the world, so often employed against religion, has really a greater value for religion than the order which is first presented to us in our study of the world and which is visible in a smaller part. The perturbations in the course of the stars point to a higher unity and a bolder combination than those we have already discovered in the regularity of their orbits. The anomalies, the idle sports of plastic Nature, compel us to see that she handles her most definite forms with free, nay capricious arbitrariness, with a fantasy the laws of which only a higher standpoint can show.

Wherefore, in the religion of the Ancients, only inferior divinities and ministering virgins had the oversight of all that recurred uniformly and had an already discovered order, but the exceptions which were not understood, the revolutions for which there was no law, were the work of the father of the gods. We also have strange, dread, mysterious emotions, when the imagination reminds us that there is more in nature than we know. They are easy to distinguish from the quiet and settled consciousness that everything is involved in the most distant combinations of the Whole, that every individual thing is determined by the yet unexplored general life. This consciousness is produced by what we understand in Nature, but I mean those dim presentiments which are the same in all, even though, as is right, only the educated seek to elucidate them and change them into a more lively activity of perception. In others, being comprehended in ignorance and misunderstanding, they grow to a delusion which we call pure superstition, under which, however, there manifestly lies a pious shudder of which we shall not be ashamed.

Furthermore, consider how you are impressed by the universal opposition of life and death. The sustained, conquering power, whereby every living thing nourishes itself, forcefully awakes the dead and enters it on a new course by drawing it into its own life. On every side we find provision prepared for all living, not lying dead, but itself alive and everywhere being reproduced. With all this multitude of forms of life, and the enormous mass of material which each uses in turn, there is enough for all. Thus each completes his course and succumbs to an inward fate and not to outward want. What a feeling of endless fulness and superabundant riches! How are we impressed by a universal paternal care and a childlike confidence that without anxiety plays away sweet life in a full and abundant world! Consider the lilies of the field, they sow not, neither do they reap, yet your Heavenly Father feedeth them, wherefore be not anxious. This happy view, this serene, easy mind was for one of the greatest heroes of religion, the fair profit of a very limited and meager communion with nature. How much more should we win who have been permitted by a richer age to go deeper!

Already we know something more of the univer-

sally distributed forces, the eternal laws, whereby individual things, that is things which have their souls in
themselves apart, in a more definite boundary, in what
we call bodies, are fashioned and destroyed. See how
attraction and repulsion, everywhere and always active, determine everything; and how all difference and
opposition are again resolved into a higher unity. Only
in appearance, can anything finite boast itself of a
separate existence. See how all likeness is concealed by
being distributed in a thousand different shapes. Nothing simple is to be found, but all is skillfully connected
and interwoven. We would see and exhort all who
share in the culture of the age to observe, how, in this
sense, the Spirit of the World reveals itself as visibly,
as completely, in small as in great, and we would not
stop with such a consciousness of it as might be had
anywhere and from anything. Even without all the
knowledge which has made our century glorious, the
World-Spirit showed itself to the most ancient sages.
Not only did they have, by intuition, the first pure
speaking image of the world, but there was kindled in
the hearts a love for nature and a joy in her, that is for
us still lovely and pleasing. Had this but penetrated
to the people, who knows what strong and lofty way
religion might have taken from the beginning? At
present it has penetrated to all who would be considered cultured. Through the gradual operation of the
fellowship between knowledge and feeling, they have
arrived at the immediate feeling that there is nothing
even in their own nature that is not a work of this
Spirit, an exhibition and application of these laws. In
virtue of this feeling, all that touches their life becomes
truly a world, a unity permeated by the Divinity that

fashions it. It is natural, therefore, that there should be in them all, that love and joy, that deep reverence for nature which made sacred the art and life of Antiquity, which was the source of that wisdom, which we have returned to and are at length beginning to commend and glorify by fruits long delayed. Such a feeling of being one with nature, of being quite rooted in it, so that in all the changing phenomena of life, even in the change between life and death itself, we might await all that should befall us with approbation and peace, as merely the working out of those eternal laws, would indeed be the germ of all the religious feelings furnished by this side of existence.

But is it so easy to find original in nature the love and resistance, the unity and peculiarity, whereby it is a Whole for us? Just because our sense tends in quite another direction, is there so little truly religious enjoyment of nature. The sense of the Whole must be first found, chiefly within our own minds, and from thence transferred to corporeal nature. Wherefore the spirit is for us not only the seat of religion but its nearest world. The Universe portrays itself in the inner life, and then the corporeal is comprehensible from the spiritual. If the mind is to produce and sustain religion it must operate upon us as a world and as in a world.

Let me reveal a secret to you that lies almost hidden in one of the oldest sources of poetry and religion. As long as the first man was alone with himself and nature, the Deity ruled over him and addressed him in various ways, but he did not understand and answered nothing. His paradise was beautiful, the stars shone down on him from a beautiful heaven, but there awoke in him no sense for the world. Even from within, this sense was not developed. Still his mind was stirred with longing for a world, and he collected the animal creation before him, if perhaps out of them a world might be formed. Then the Deity recognized that the world would be nothing, as long as man was alone. He created a helpmate for him. At length the deep-toned harmonies awoke in him, and the world fashioned itself before his eyes. In flesh of his flesh, and bone of his bone, he discovered humanity. In this first love he had a foretaste of all love's forms and tendencies—in humanity he found the world. From this moment he was capable of seeing and hearing the voice of the Deity, and even the most insolent transgression of His laws did not any more shut him out from intercourse with the Eternal Being.

The history of us all is related in this sacred legend. All is present in vain for those who set themselves alone. In order to receive the life of the World-Spirit, and have religion, man must first, in love, and through love, have found humanity. Wherefore, humanity and religion are closely and indissolubly united. A longing for love, ever satisfied and ever again renewed, forthwith becomes religion. Each man embraces most warmly the person in whom the world mirrors itself for him most clearly and purely; he loves most tenderly the person whom he believes combines all he lacks of a complete manhood. Similarly the pious feelings are most holy that express for him existence in the whole of humanity, whether as blessedness in attaining or of need in coming short.

Wherefore, to find the most glorious elements of religion, let us enter upon the territory where you are in your peculiar, your most loved home. Here your inner life had its birth, here you see the goal of all your striving and doing before your eyes, and here you feel the growth of your powers whereby you are evermore conducted towards it. Humanity is for you the true universe, and the rest is only added in so far as it is related to it or forms its surroundings. Even for me, this point of view suffices. Yet it has often pained me that, with all your interest in humanity, and with all your zeal for it, you are always in difficulties with it, and divided from it, and pure love cannot become right prominent in you. Each of you in his own way harasses himself to improve it, and to educate it, and what will not come to an issue you finally cast aside in dejection.

I make bold to say, that this also comes from your lack of religion. You wish to work on humanity, and you select men, individuals for contemplation. They displease you vastly. Among the thousand possible causes, unquestionably that which is finest in itself, and which belongs to the best of you, is that you are, in your own way, far too ethical. You take men singly, and you have an ideal of the individual to which no one corresponds. If you would begin with religion, you would have far more success. If you would only attempt to exchange the objects of your working and the objects of your contemplation! Work on individuals, but rise in contemplation, on the wings of religion, to endless, undivided humanity. Seek this humanity in each individual; regard the nature of every person as one revelation of it, and of all that now oppresses you no trace would remain. I at least boast myself of a moral disposition, I know how to value human excellence, and commonness could almost overwhelm me with the unpleasant feeling of contempt, were it not that religion gives me a great and glorious view of all.

Just consider what a consummate artist the Genius of humanity is. It can make nothing that has not a nature of its own. As soon as it assays its brush, or sharpens its pencil, there appear living and significant features. It imagines and fashions countless forms. Millions wear the costume of the time, and are faithful pictures of its necessities and its tastes. In others there are memories of the past, or presentiments of a distant future. Some are most lofty and striking types of the fairest and divinest, others resemble grotesques produced in the most original and fleeting mood of a master. The common view, based on a misunderstanding of the sacred words that there are vessels of honor and vessels of dishonor, is not pious. Only by comparing details could such an opposition appear to you. You must not contemplate anything alone, you must rather rejoice in everything in its own place. All that we can be conscious of at once, all, as it were, that stands on one sheet, presents one movement of the complete working of the Whole, and belongs, as it were, to one great historical picture. Would you make light of the chief groups that give life and affluence to the Whole? Should not each heavenly form be glorified in having a thousand others that regard it and are related to it, bowing before it? Indeed, there is more in this presentation than a mere simile. Eternal humanity is unweariedly active, seeking to step forth from its inward, mysterious existence into the light, and to present itself in the most varied way, in the fleeting manifestation of the endless life. That is the harmony of the Universe, the wondrous and unparalleled unity of that eternal work of art. . . .

What would the uniform repetition of even a highest ideal be? Mankind, time and circumstances excepted, would be identical. They would be the same formula with a different coefficient. What would it be in comparison with the endless variety which humanity does manifest? . . .

This oft-bewailed superfluity of the commonest forms of humanity, ever returning unchanged in a thousand copies, does not disturb the pious mind. The Eternal Mind commands that the forms in which individuality is most difficult to discern, should stand closest together, and even the finite mind can see the reason why. And each has something of its own, and no two are identical. In every life there is some moment, like the coruscation of baser metals, when, by the approach of something higher, or by some electric shock, it surpasses itself and stands on the highest pinnacle of its possibilities. For this moment it was created, in this moment it fulfilled its purpose, and, after this moment its exhausted vitality again subsides. To call forth this moment in ordinary souls and to contemplate them during it is a pleasure to be envied, and to those who have not known it, the whole existence of them must appear superfluous and despicable.

Yet the existence of such an ordinary soul has a double meaning in respect of the Whole. If I arrest in thought the course of that unresting machinery whereby all that is human is woven together and made interdependent, I see that each individual in his inner nature is a necessary complement of a complete intuition of humanity. One shows me how any fragment, if only the plastic impulse of the Whole still quickens it, can calmly progress, fashioning itself in graceful, regular forms; another how, from want of a vivifying and combining warmth, the hardness of the earthly material cannot be overcome; while, in a third, I see how, in an atmosphere too violently agitated, the spirit within is disturbed in its working, so that nothing comes clearly and recognizably to light. One appears as the rude and animal portion of mankind, stirred only by the first ungainly motions of humanity; another is the pure dematerialized spirit that, having been separated from all that is base and unworthy, hovers with noiseless foot over the earth. But everything between also has a purpose. It shows how, in the minute detached phenomena of individual lives, the different elements of human nature all appear at every stage and in every manner. It is not enough that among this countless multitude there are always a few at least who are the distinguished representatives of humanity, who strike different melodious chords that require no further accompaniment, and no subsequent explication, but who, in the one note, charm and satisfy by their harmony the whole soul. But even the noblest only presents mankind in one way and in one of its movements, and in some sense everyone is a peculiar exhibition of humanity and does the same thing, and were a single figure to fail in the great picture, it would be impossible to comprehend it completely and perfectly. . . .

Do I, on the other hand, observe the eternal wheels of humanity in motion, this vast interaction, nothing moved by itself, nothing moving only itself, I am greatly quieted about the other side of your complaint,

that reason and soul, sensuality and morality, understanding and blind force appear in such separate masses.
Why do you see things singly that are not single and
do not work by themselves? The reason of one and
the disposition of another have as strong a mutual influence as if they were in one and the same subject. . . .
The outlines of personality which appear to you so
definite, from my standpoint, dissolve. The magic
circle of prevailing opinions and infectious feelings surrounds all and plays around all like an atmosphere filled
with dissolving and magnetic forces. By the most vital
diffusion it smelts all things, even the most distant, into
a single activity, the issue of which is to impel those
who are really in possession of light and truth to activity, so that some are deeply influenced, and others
have at least a superficial illumination, brilliant and
deceptive.

In this connection of everything with the sphere
to which it belongs and in which it has significance all
is good and divine, and a fulness of joy and peace is
the feeling of those who allow all things to work upon
them in this great connection. But they will also feel
how contemplation isolates single things in single moments. The common impulse of men, who know nothing of this dependence, is to seize and retain this and
that, to hedge in their Ego and to surround it with
manifold outworks. They seek to conduct their own
existence according to their own self-will and not be
disturbed by the eternal current of the world. . . .

From these wanderings through the whole territory of humanity, pious feeling returns, quickened and
educated, into its own Ego, and there finds all the influences that had streamed upon it from the most dis-

tant regions. If, on returning with the consecration of intercourse with the world still fresh upon us, we give heed how it is with us in this feeling, we become conscious that our Ego vanishes, not only into smallness and insignificance, but into one-sidedness, insufficiency and nothingness. What lies nearer to mortal man than unaffected humility? And when gradually our feeling becomes quick and alert to what there is in the path of humanity that sustains and forwards, and what, on the contrary, must sooner or later be conquered and destroyed, if it is not recast and transformed, and when from this law we regard all doings in the world, what is more natural than deep contrition for all in us that is hostile to human nature, the submissive desire to conciliate the Deity, and the most earnest longing to put ourselves and all that belongs to us in safety in that sacred region where alone there is security against death and destruction? Advancing further, we perceive how the Whole only becomes clear to us, how we only reach intuition of it and unity with it in fellowship with others, by the influence of those who have long been freed from dependence on their own fleeting being, and from the endeavor to expand and isolate it. How, then, can we avoid a feeling of special affinity to those whose actions have defended our existence, and happily guided it through threatening dangers? Though by us they become conscious of their life in the Whole, we honor them as those who, before us, have reached this union.

Not by examples which are rare, but by passing through these and similar feelings you discover in yourselves the outlines of the fairest and the basest, the noblest and the most despicable. . . . In your own order, you have actually passed through all those different forms. You are a compendium of humanity. In a certain sense your single nature embraces all human nature. Your Ego, being multiplied and more clearly outlined, is in all its smallest and swiftest changes immortalized in the manifestations of human nature. As soon as this is seen, you can love yourselves with a pure and blameless love. Humility, that never forsakes you, has its counterpart in the feeling that the whole of humanity lives and works in you. Even contrition is sweetened to joyful self-sufficiency. This is the completion of religion on this side. It works its way back to the heart, and there finds the Infinite. The man in whom this is accomplished, is no more in need of a mediator for any sort of intuition of humanity. Rather he is himself a mediator for many.

But there is not merely the swinging of feeling between the world and the individual, in the present moment. Except as something going on, we cannot comprehend what affects us, and we cannot comprehend ourselves, except as thus progressively affected. Wherefore, as feeling persons, we are ever driven back into the past. The spirit furnishes the chief nourishment for our piety, and history immediately and especially is for religion the richest source. History is not of value for religion, because it hastens or controls in any way the progress of humanity in its development, but because it is the greatest and most general revelation of the deepest and holiest. In this sense, however, religion begins and ends with history. Prophecy and history are for religion the same and indistinguishable, and all true history has at first had a religious purpose, and has taken its departure from religious ideas.

What is finest and tenderest in history, moreover, cannot be communicated scientifically, but can only be comprehended in the feeling of a religious disposition. . . . Peoples and generations of mortals appear as all alike necessary for the completeness of history, though, like individuals, of different worth. Some are estimable and spirited, and work strongly without ceasing, permeating space and defying time. Others are common and insignificant, fitted only to show some peculiar shade of some single form of life. For one moment only they are really living and noticeable. One thought they exhibit, one conception they produce, and then they hasten towards destruction that the power that produced them may be given to something else. As vegetable nature, from the destruction of whole species, and from the ruins of whole generations of plants, produces and nourishes a new race, so spiritual nature rears from the ruins of a glorious and beautiful world of men, a new world that draws its first vital strength from elements decomposed and wondrously transformed. Being deeply impressed with this sense of a universal connection, your glance perhaps passes so often directly from least to greatest and greatest to least, going backwards and forwards, till through dizziness it can neither distinguish great nor small, cause nor effect, preservation nor destruction. This state continues, and then that well-known figure of an eternal fate appears. Its features bear the impress of this state, being a marvelous mixture of obstinate self-will and deep wisdom, of rude unfeeling force and heartfelt love, of which first one seizes you and then another, now inviting you to impotent defiance and now to childlike submission.

Penetrate further and compare this partial striving of the individual, the fruit of opposing views, with the quiet uniform course of the Whole. You will see how the high World-Spirit smilingly marches past all that furiously opposes him. You will see how dread Nemesis, never wearied, follows his steps, meting out punishment to the haughty who resist the gods. Even the stoutest and choicest who have with steadfastness, worthy perhaps of praise and wonder, refused to bow before the gentle breath of the great Spirit, it mows down with iron hand. Would you comprehend the proper character of all changes and of all human progress, a feeling resting on history must show you more surely than aught else, that living gods rule who hate nothing so much as death, and that nothing is to be persecuted and destroyed like this first and last foe of the spirit. The rude, the barbarian, the formless are to be absorbed and recast. Nothing is to be a dead mass that moves only by impact and resists only by unconscious collision; all is to be individual, connected, complex, exalted life. Blind instinct, unthinking custom, dull obedience, everything lazy and passive, all those sad symptoms of the death slumber of freedom and humanity are to be abolished. To this the work of the minutes and the centuries is directed, it is the great ever advancing work of redemptive love.

Some prominent emotions of religion connected with nature and humanity I have now sketched in vague outline. I have brought you to the limits of your horizon. Here is the end and summit of religion for all to whom humanity is the whole world. But consider that in your feeling there is something that despises these bounds, something in virtue of which you cannot stay where you are. Beyond this point only infinity is to be looked into. I will not speak of the presentiments which define themselves and become thoughts which might by subtilty be established, that humanity, being capable of motion and cultivation, being not only differently manifested in the individual, but here and there really being different, cannot possibly be the highest, the sole manifestation of the unity of spirit and matter. As the individual is only one form of humanity, so humanity may be only one form of this unity. Beside it many other similar forms may exist, bounding it and standing over against it. But in our own feeling we all find something similar. The dependence of our earth, and therefore of the highest unity it has produced, upon other worlds, has been impressed upon us both by nature and by education. Hence this ever active but seldom understood presentiment of some other marriage of spirit and matter, visible and finite, but above humanity, higher and closer and productive of more beautiful forms. But any sketch that could be drawn would be too definite. Any echo of the feeling could only be fleeting and vague. Hence it is exposed to misconception and is so often taken for folly and superstition. . . .

This is the rank of religion, as the sum of all higher feelings. That it alone removes man from one-sidedness and narrowness I have already indicated. Now I am in a position to be more definite. In all activity and working, be it moral or artistic, man must strive for mastery. But when man becomes quite absorbed, all mastery limits and chills, and makes him one-sided and hard. The mind is directed chiefly to one point, and this one point cannot satisfy it. Can man, by advancing from one narrow work to another, really use his whole power? Will not the larger part be unused, and turn, in consequence, against himself and devour him? How many of you go to ruin because you are too great for yourselves? A superfluity of power and impulse that never issues in any work, because there is no work adequate, drives you aimlessly about, and is your destruction.

To resist this evil would you have those who are too great for one object of human endeavor, unite them all —art, science, life, and any others you may know of? This would simply be your old desire to have humanity complete everywhere, your ever recurring love of uniformity. But is it possible? Those objects, as soon as they are attended to separately, all alike strive to rouse and dominate the mind. Each tendency is directed to a work that should be completed, it has an ideal to be copied, a totality to be embraced. This rivalry of several objects of endeavor can only end by one expelling the others. Nay, even within this one sphere, the more eminent a mastery a man would attain, the more he must restrict himself. But if this preeminence entirely occupy him, and if he lives only to attain it, how shall he duly participate in the world, and how shall his life become a whole? Hence most virtuosos are one-sided and defective, or at least, outside of their own sphere, they sink into an inferior kind of life.

The only remedy is for each man, while he is definitely active in some one department, to allow himself, without definite activity, to be affected by the Infinite. In every species of religious feeling he will then become conscious of all that lies beyond the department which he directly cultivates. The Infinite is near to

everyone, for whatever be the object you have chosen
for your deliberate technical working, it does not demand much thought to advance from it to find the
Universe. In it you discover the rest as precept, or inspiration or revelation. The only way of acquiring
what lies outside the direction of the mind we have
selected, is to enjoy and comprehend it thus as a whole,
not by will as art, but by instinct for the Universe as
religion.

Even in the religious form these objects again fall
into rivalry. This result of human imperfection causes
religion to appear dismembered. Religion takes the
form of some peculiar receptivity and taste for art,
philosophy or morality, and is consequently often mistaken. Oftener, I say, it appears thus than freed from
all participation in one-sidedness, than completed, all-
embracing. Yet this complete form of religion remains
the highest, and it is only by it, that, with satisfactory
result, man sets alongside of the finite that he specially
concentrates on, an Infinite; alongside of the contract-
ing endeavor for something definite and complete, ex-
pansive soaring in the Whole and the Inexhaustible. In
this way he restores the balance and harmony of his
nature, which would be lost for ever, if, without at the
same time having religion, he abandon himself to one
object, were it the most beautiful, most splendid. A
man's special calling is the melody of his life, and it remains a simple, meager series of notes unless religion,
with its endlessly rich variety, accompany it with all
notes, and raise the simple song to a full-voiced, glorious harmony.

If then this, that I trust I have indicated clearly
enough for you all, is really the nature of religion, I

have already answered the questions, Whence do those dogmas and doctrines come that many consider the essence of religion? Where do they properly belong? And how do they stand related to what is essential in religion? They are all the result of that contemplation of feeling, of that reflection and comparison, of which we have already spoken. The conceptions that underlie these propositions are, like your conceptions from experience, nothing but general expressions for definite feelings. They are not necessary for religion itself, scarcely even for communicating religion, but reflection requires and creates them. Miracle, inspiration, revelation, supernatural intimations, much piety can be had without the need of any one of these conceptions. But when feeling is made the subject of reflection and comparison they are absolutely unavoidable. In this sense all these conceptions do certainly belong to the sphere of religion, and indeed belong without condition or the smallest limit to their application.

The strife about what event is properly a miracle, and wherein its character properly consists, how much revelation there may be and how far and for what reasons man may properly believe in it, and the manifest endeavor to deny and set aside as much as can be done with decency and consideration, in the foolish notion that philosophy and reason are served thereby, is one of the childish operations of the metaphysicians and moralists in religion. They confuse all points of view and bring religion into discredit, as if it trespassed on the universal validity of scientific and physical conclusions. . . . Religion, however loudly it may demand back all those well abused conceptions, leaves your physics untouched, and please God, also your psychology.

What is a miracle? What we call miracle is everywhere else called sign, indication. Our name, which means a wonder, refers purely to the mental condition of the observer. . . . Every finite thing, however, is a sign of the Infinite, and so these various expressions declare the immediate relation of a phenomenon to the Infinite and the Whole. But does that involve that every event should not have quite as immediate a relation to the finite and to nature? Miracle is simply the religious name for event. Every event, even the most natural and usual, becomes a miracle, as soon as the religious view of it can be the dominant. To me all is miracle. In your sense the inexplicable and strange alone is miracle, in mine it is no miracle. The more religious you are, the more miracle would you see everywhere. . . .

What is revelation? Every original and new communication of the Universe to man is a revelation, as, for example, every such moment of conscious insight as I have just referred to. Every intuition and every original feeling proceeds from revelation. As revelation lies beyond consciousness, demonstration is not possible, yet we are not merely to assume it generally, but each one knows best himself what is repeated and learned elsewhere, and what is original and new. . . .

What is inspiration? It is simply the general expression for the feeling of true morality and freedom. But do not mistake me. It is not that marvelous and much-praised morality and freedom that accompany and embellish actions with deliberations. It is that action which springs from the heart of man, despite, or at least, regardless of, all external occasion. . . .

What is operation of grace? Nothing else manifestly than the common expression for revelation and inspiration, for interchange between the entrance of the world into man, through intuition and feeling, and the outgoing of man into the world, through action and culture. It includes both, in their originality and in their divine character, so that the whole life of the pious simply forms a series of operations of divine grace.

You see that all these ideas, in so far as religion requires, or can adopt ideas, are the first and the most essential. They indicate in the most characteristic manner a man's consciousness of his religion, because they indicate just what necessarily and universally must be in it. The man who does not see miracles of his own from the standpoint from which he contemplates the world, the man in whose heart no revelation of his own arises, when his soul longs to draw in the beauty of the world, and to be permeated by its spirit; the man who does not, in supreme moments, feel, with the most lively assurance, that a divine spirit urges him, and that he speaks and acts from holy inspiration, has no religion. . . .

Belief, on the contrary, usually so called, which is to accept what another has said or done, or to wish to think and feel as another has thought and felt, is a hard and base service. So far is it from being the highest in religion, as is asserted, that it must be rejected by all who would force their way into the sanctuary of religion. To wish to have and hold a faith that is an echo, proves that a man is incapable of religion; to demand it of others, shows that there is no understanding of religion. You wish always to stand on your own feet and go your own way, and this worthy intent should not scare you from religion.

Religion is no slavery, no captivity, least of all for your reason. You must belong to yourselves. Indeed, this is an indispensable condition of having any part in religion.

Every man, a few choice souls excepted, does, to be sure, require a guide to lead and stimulate, to wake his religious sense from its first slumber, and to give it its first direction. But this you accord to all powers and functions of the human soul, and why not to this one? . . . You are right in despising the wretched echoes who derive their religion entirely from another, or depend on a dead writing, swearing by it and proving out of it.

Every sacred writing is in itself a glorious production, a speaking monument from the heroic time of religion, but, through servile reverence, it would become merely a mausoleum, a monument that a great spirit once was there, but is now no more. Did this spirit still live and work, he would look with love, and with a feeling of equality upon his work which yet could only be a weaker impress of himself. Not every person has religion who believes in a sacred writing, but only the man who has a lively and immediate understanding of it, and who, therefore, so far as he himself is concerned, could most easily do without it. . . .

I have tried, as best I could, therefore, to show you what religion really is. Have you found anything therein unworthy of you, nay, of the highest human culture? Must you not rather long all the more for that universal union with the world which is only possible through feeling, the more you are separated and isolated by definite culture and individuality? Have you not often felt this holy longing, as something unknown? Become conscious of the call of your deepest nature and follow it, I conjure you. Banish the false shame of a century which should not determine you but should be made and determined by you. Return to what lies so near to you, yes, even to you, the violent separation from which cannot fail to destroy the most beautiful part of your nature.

It appears to me, however, that many among you do not believe that I can here mean to end my present business. How can I have spoken thoroughly of the nature of religion, seeing I have not treated at all of immortality, and of God only a little in passing? . . .

But I am not of your opinion. First of all, I do not believe I have said nothing about immortality and so little about God. Both, I believe, are in all and in everything that I have adduced as an element of religion. Had I not presupposed God and immortality I could not have said what I have said, for, only what is divine and immortal has room in which to speak of religion.

In the second place, just as little do I consider that I have the right to hold the conceptions and doctrines of God and of immortality, as they are usually understood, to be the principal things in religion. Only what in either is feeling and immediate consciousness, can belong to religion. God and immortality, however, as they are found in such doctrines, are ideas. How many among you—possibly most of you—are firmly convinced of one or other or both of those doctrines, without being on that account pious or having religion. As ideas they can have no greater value in religion than ideas generally. . . .

Remember in the first place that any feeling is not an emotion of piety because in it a single object as such affects us, but only in so far as in it and along with it, it affects us as revelation of God. It is, therefore, not an individual or finite thing, but God, in whom alone the particular thing is one and all, that enters our life. Nor do we stand over against the World and in it at the same time by any one faculty, but by our whole being. The divine in us, therefore, is immediately affected and called forth by the feeling. Seeing then that I have presented nothing but just this immediate and original existence of God in us through feeling, how can anyone say that I have depicted a religion without God? Is not God the highest, the only unity? Is it not God alone before whom and in whom all particular things disappear? And if you see the world as a Whole, a Universe, can you do it otherwise than in God? If not, how could you distinguish the highest existence, the original and eternal Being from a temporal and derived individual? Otherwise than by the emotions produced in us by the world we do not claim to have God in our feeling, and consequently I have not said more of Him.

If you will not admit that this is to have God, and to be conscious of Him, I can neither teach nor direct you farther. How much you may know I do not judge, for it does not at present concern me, but in respect of feeling and sentiment, you would be for me godless. Science, it is true, is extolled as giving an immediate knowledge about God, that is the source of all other knowledge; only we are not now speaking of science, but of religion. This way of knowing about God which most praise and which I also am to laud, is neither the idea of God as the undivided unity and source of all, that is placed by you at the head of all knowledge; nor is it the feeling of God in the heart, of which we boast ourselves. It lags far behind the demands of science, and is for piety something quite subordinate. It is an idea compounded from characteristics, from what are called attributes of God. These attributes correspond to the different ways in which the unity of the individual and the Whole, expresses itself in feeling. Hence I can only say of this idea, what I have said of ideas generally, in reference to religion, that there can be much piety without it, and that it is first formed when piety is made an object of contemplation.

Yet this idea of God, as it is usually conceived, is different from the other ideas before adduced, for though it seeks to be the highest and to stand above all, God, being thought of as too like us, as a thinking and willing Person, is drawn down into the region of opposition. It therefore appears natural that the more like man God is conceived, the more easily another mode of presentation is set over against it. Hence, we have an idea of the Highest Being, not as personally thinking and willing, but exalted above all personality, as the universal, productive, connecting necessity for all thought and existence.

Nothing seems to me less fitting than for the adherents of the former view to charge with godlessness those who, in dread of this anthropomorphism, take refuge in the other, or for the adherents of this latter view to make the humanness of the idea of God a ground for charging the adherents of the former with idolatry, or for declaring their piety void.

It matters not what conceptions a man adheres to, he can still be pious. His piety, the divine in his feeling, may be better than his conception, and his desire to place the essence of piety in conception, only makes him misunderstand himself. Consider how narrow is the presentation of God in the one conception, and how dead and rigid in the other. Neither corresponds to its object, and thus cannot be a proof of piety, except in so far as it rests on something in the mind, of which it has come far short. Rightly understood, both present, at least, one element of feeling, but, without feeling, neither is of any value. Many believe in and accept a God presented in conception, and yet are nothing less than pious, and in no case is this conception the germ from which their piety could ever spring, for it has no life in itself. Neither conception is any sign of a perfect or of an imperfect religion, but perfection and imperfection depend upon the degree of cultivation of the religious sense. . . .

But we have here the old confusion, the unmistakable sign of defective culture. Those who are at the same stage, only not at the same point, are most strongly repudiated. The proper standard of religiousness, that which announces the stage to which a man has attained, is his sense for the Deity. But to which idea he will attach himself depends purely on what he requires it for, and whether his imagination chiefly inclines towards existence and nature or consciousness and thought.

You will not, I trust, consider it blasphemy or incongruity that such a matter should depend on the direction of the imagination. By imagination I do not mean anything subordinate or confused, but the highest and most original faculty in man. All else in the human mind is simply reflection upon it, and is therefore dependent on it. Imagination in this sense is the free generation of thoughts, whereby you come to a conception of the world; such a conception you cannot receive from without, nor compound from inferences. From this conception you are then impressed with the feeling of omnipotence. The subsequent translation into thought depends on whether one is willing in the consciousness of his own weakness to be lost in the mysterious obscurity, or whether, first of all, seeking definiteness of thought, he cannot think of anything except under the one form given to us, that of consciousness or self-consciousness. Recoil from the obscurity of indefinite thought is the one tendency of the imagination, recoil from the appearance of contradiction in transferring the forms of the finite to the Infinite is the other.

Now cannot the same inwardness of religion be combined with both? Would not a closer consideration show that the two ways of conceiving are not very wide apart? But the pantheistic idea is not to be thought of as death, and no effort is to be spared to surpass in thought the limits of the personal idea. . . .

This now brings me to the second point, to immortality. I cannot conceal that in the usual manner of treating this subject there is still more that seems to me inconsistent with the nature of piety. I believe I have just shown you in what way each one bears in himself an unchangeable and eternal nature. If our feeling nowhere attaches itself to the individual, but if its content is our relation to God wherein all that is individual and fleeting disappears, there can be nothing fleeting in it, but all must be eternal. In the religious life then we may well say we have already offered up and disposed of all that is mortal, and that we actually are enjoying immortality. But the immortality that most men imagine and their longing for it, seem to me irreligious, nay, quite opposed to the spirit of piety. Dislike to the very aim of religion is the ground of their wish to be immortal. Recall how religion earnestly strives to expand the sharply cut outline of personality. Gradually they are to be lost in the Infinite that we, becoming conscious of the Universe, may as much as possible be one with it. But men struggle against this aim. They are anxious about their personality, and do not wish to overstep the accustomed limit or to be anything else but a manifestation of it. The one opportunity that death gives them of transcending it, they are very far from wishing to embrace. On the contrary, they are concerned as to how they are to carry it with them beyond this life, and their utmost endeavor is for longer sight and better limbs. But God speaks to them as it stands written, "Whosoever loses his life for my sake, the same shall keep it, and whosoever keeps it, the same shall lose it." The life that they would keep is one that cannot be kept. If their concern is with the eternity of their single person, why are they not as anxious about what it has been as about what it is to be? What does forwards avail when they cannot go backwards? They desire an immortality that is no immortality. They are not even capable of comprehending it, for who can endure the effort to conceive an endless temporal existence? Thereby they lose the immortality they could always have, and their mortal life in addition, by thoughts that distress and torture them in vain. Would they but attempt to surrender their lives from love to God! Would they but strive to annihilate their personality and to live in the One and in the All! Whosoever has learned to be more than himself, knows that he loses little when he loses himself. Only the man who denying himself sinks himself in as much of the whole Universe as he can attain, and in whose soul a greater and holier longing has arisen, has a right to the hopes that death gives. With him alone it is really possible to hold further converse about the endlessness to which, through death, we infallibly soar.

This then is my view of these subjects. The usual conception of God as one single being outside of the world and behind the world is not the beginning and the end of religion. . . . The true nature of religion is neither this idea nor any other, but immediate consciousness of the Deity as He is found in ourselves and in the world. Similarly the goal and character of the religious life is not the immortality desired and believed in by many. . . . It is the immortality which we can now have in this temporal life; it is the problem in the solution of which we are for ever to be engaged. In the midst of finitude to be one with the Infinite and in every moment to be eternal is the immortality of religion.

THIRD SPEECH

The Cultivation of Religion

As I MYSELF have willingly confessed, the endeavor to make proselytes from unbelievers is deep rooted in the character of religion. Yet that is not what now urges me to speak to you of the cultivation of man for this noble capacity. For this cultivation we believers know of only one means—the free expression and communication of religion. When religion moves in a man with all its native force, when it carries every faculty of his spirit imperiously along in the stream of its impulse, we expect it to penetrate into the hearts of all who live and breathe within its influence. Every corresponding element being stirred by this life-giving power, they should attain a consciousness of their existence, and the attentive ear should be gladdened by an answering note of kindred sound. Where the pious person fails to awake a life like his by the natural expression of his own life, he will despise nobly every strange charm, every exercise of force, in the calm conviction that the time has not yet come for anything congenial to appear. . . .

Everyone of us misses in himself not a little that belongs to a complete humanity, and many lack much. What wonder, then, if the number in whom religion

refuses to develop should be great! Necessarily it
must be great, else how could we come to see it in—
if I might so say—its incarnate, historical existence,
or discern the bounds it sets on all sides to the other
capacities of man, or how by them again it is in manifold ways bounded. Or how should we know how far
man can anywhere succeed without it, and where it
sustains him and forwards him; or guess that, without
his knowledge, it is busy in him.

But especially in these times of universal confusion and upheaval, it is natural that its slumbering
spark should not glow up in many. . . . In such a
state of things it would be foolish to expect that many
could be fit to cultivate and retain religious feelings
which prosper best in quiet. In the midst of this fer-
ment, indeed, the aspect of the moral world is more
majestic and noble than ever, and at moments there
are hints of more significant traits than ever before
in the centuries. Yet who can rescue himself from
the universal turmoil? Who can escape the power
of narrower interests? Who has calm enough to stand
still, and steadfastness enough for undisturbed contemplation?

But suppose the happiest times and suppose the
best will, not only to arouse by communication the
capacity for religion where it does exist, but, by every
possible way, to ingraft and to impart it. Where,
then, is there such a way? All that the activity
and art of one man can do for another is to communicate conceptions to be the basis of thoughts,
and so far to associate them with his own ideas
that they may be remembered at fitting times. But
no one can arrive at the point of making others

think what thoughts he will. There is a contrariety that cannot be eliminated from words, and much less can you get beyond this means and freely produce what inner activity you will. In short, on the mechanism of the spirit everyone can, in some measure, work, but into its organization, into the sacred workshop of the Universe, no one can enter at pleasure. No one can change or disarrange, take from or add to. At the most he may, by means of this mechanism, retard the development of the spirit. Part of the growth may thus be violently mutilated, but nothing can be molded. From this sanctuary of his organization which force cannot enter, all that pertains to the true life of man, all that should be an ever alert, operative impulse in him, proceeds.

And such is religion. In the spirit it inhabits it is uninterruptedly active and strong, making everything an object for itself and turning every thought and action into a theme for its heavenly fantasy. Like everything else, then, that should be ever present, ever active in the human soul, it lies far beyond the domain of teaching and imparting. Instruction in religion, meaning that piety itself is teachable, is absurd and unmeaning. Our opinions and doctrines we can indeed communicate, if we have words and our hearers have the comprehending, imagining power of the understanding. But we know very well that those things are only the shadows of our religious emotions, and if our pupils do not share our emotions, even though they do understand the thought, they have no possession that can truly repay their toil. This retreat into oneself, there to perceive oneself, cannot be taught. Even the most inspired person who can see,

it matters not before what object he finds himself,
the original light of the Universe, cannot by the word
of instruction transfer this power and dexterity to
another. . . .

Of course there is in religion a mastership and
a discipleship. But this attachment is no blind imitation. It is not the master that makes disciples, but
he is their master because of their choice. And if,
by the utterance of our own religion, religion is
awakened in others, we cannot retain it in our power
or attach it to ourselves. As soon as it lives, their
religion also is free and goes its own way. On blazing
up in the soul, the sacred spark spreads to a free and
living flame, fed by its own atmosphere. More or less
it illumines for the soul the whole circuit of the
world, so that, following his own impulse, he may
settle far away from the place where first the new
life was lit. Compelled simply by the feeling of
weakness and finitude, by an original, inward determination to settle in some definite quarter, without
being ungrateful to his first guide, he makes choice
of that climate which suits him best. There he seeks
for himself a center, and moving self-limited in his
new course, of his own choice and spontaneous liking,
he calls himself the disciple of him who first settled
in this dear spot and showed its splendor.

I do not, therefore, aim at training either you or
others to religion. Nor would I teach you by resolve
or rule to train yourselves. I would not leave the
sphere of religion—as by doing so I would—but a
little longer I would tarry with you within. The
Universe itself trains its own observers and admirers,

and how that comes to pass we shall now see, as far as it can be seen.

You know how each element of humanity discloses itself by the place it maintains against the others. By this universal strife everything in every man attains a determinate form and size. Now this strife is only sustained by the fellowship of the single elements, by the movement of the Whole. Hence every man and every thing in every man is a work of the Whole. This is the only way in which the pious sense can conceive man. . . .

Man is born with the religious capacity as with every other. If only his sense for the profoundest depths of his own nature is not crushed out, if only all fellowship between himself and the Primal Source is not quite shut off, religion would, after its own fashion, infallibly be developed. But in our time, alas! that is exactly what, in very large measure, does happen. With pain I see daily how the rage for calculating and explaining suppresses the sense. I see how all things unite to bind man to the finite, and to a very small portion of the finite, that the infinite may as far as possible vanish from his eyes.

What hinders the prosperity of religion? Not you, not the doubters and scoffers. Even though you were all of one mind to have no religion, you would not disturb Nature in her purpose of producing piety from the depths of the soul, for your influence could only later find prepared soil. Nor, as is supposed, do the immoral most hinder the prosperity of religion, for it is quite a different power to which their endeavors are opposed. But the discreet and practical

men of today are, in the present state of the world,
the foes of religion, and their great preponderance
is the cause why it plays such a poor and insignificant
role, for from tender childhood they maltreat man,
crushing out his higher aspirations.

With great reverence I regard the longing of
young minds for the marvelous and supernatural.
Joyfully taking in the motley show of things, they
seek at the same time something else to set over against
it. They search everywhere for something surpassing
the accustomed phenomena and the light play of life.
However many earthly objects are presented for their
knowing, there seems still another sense unnourished.
That is the first stirrings of religion. A secret, inexplicable presentiment urges them past the riches
of this world. . . . True, it is a delusion to seek the
Infinite immediately outside of the finite, but is it
not natural in those who know but the surface of
even the finite and sensuous? Is it not the delusion
of whole peoples and whole schools of wisdom?

Were there but guardians of religion among
those who care for the young, how easily could this
natural error be corrected! And, in clearer times, how
greedily would young souls then abandon themselves
to the impressions of the Infinite in its omnipresence!

It were even better if life were left quietly to
take its own course. Let it be supposed that the taste
for grotesque figures is as natural to the young imagination in religion as in art, and let it be richly
satisfied. Have no anxiety when the earnest and
sacred mythology, that is considered the very essence
of religion, is immediately united with the careless
games of childhood. Suppose that the Heavenly

Father, the Savior, the angels are but another kind of fairies and sylphs. In many, perhaps, the foundation may be laid for an insufficient and dead letter. While the images grow pale, the word, as the empty frame in which they have been fixed, may remain hanging. But man, thus treated, would be more left to himself, and a right-thinking, uncorrupted soul that knew how to keep himself free from the titillation of scraping and scheming, would more easily find, in due time, the natural issue from this labyrinth.

Now, on the contrary, that tendency is, from the beginning, forcibly suppressed. Everything mysterious and marvelous is proscribed. Imagination is not to be filled with airy images! It is just as easy to store the memory with real objects and to be preparing for life! Poor young souls, desiring quite other fare, are wearied with moral tales and have to learn how beautiful and necessary it is to be genteel and discreet. The current conceptions of things that they would of themselves have encountered soon enough, are impressed upon them, as if it were an urgent business that could never be too soon accomplished. Without regard to their real want, there is given them that of which far too soon there will be too much.

In proportion as man must busy himself in a narrow way with a single object, to rescue the universality of the sense an impulse awakes in everyone to allow the dominating activity and all its kindred to rest, and to open all organs to the influence of all impressions. By a secret and most helpful sympathy this impulse is strongest when the general life reveals itself most clearly in our own breasts and in the surrounding world. But to yield to this impulse in comfortable inactivity cannot be permitted, for, from the middle-class standpoint, it would be laziness and idling. In everything there must be design and aim; somewhat has always to be performed, and if the spirit can no more serve, the body must be exercised. Work and play, but no quiet, submissive contemplation!

But most of all, men are to be taught to analyze and explain. By this explaining they are completely cheated of their sense, for, as it is conducted, it is absolutely opposed to any perceptive sense. *Sense* of its own accord seeks objects for itself, it advances to meet them and it offers to embrace them. It communicates something to them which distinguishes them as its possession, its work.

It will find and be found. But this *explaining* knows nothing of this living acquisition, of this illuminating truth, of the true spirit of discovery in childlike intuition. But from first to last, objects are to be transcribed accurately in thought as something simply given. . . . Take them, then, only as life brings them, and understand that and nothing more. But to seek for yourselves and to wish to have living intercourse with things is eccentric and high-flown. It is a vain endeavor, availing nothing in human life, where things are only to be seen and handled as they have already presented themselves.

Fruitful in human life this endeavor is not, except that, without it, an active life, resting on true inward culture, is not to be found. The sense strives to comprehend the undivided impress of something whole; it will perceive what each thing is and how it is; it will know everything in its peculiar character. But that is not what they mean by understanding. What and how are too remote for them, around whence and to what end, they eternally circle. They seek to grasp nothing in and for itself, but only in special aspects, and therefore, not as a whole, but only piecemeal. To inquire or thoroughly examine whether the object they would understand is a whole, would lead them too far. Were this their desire, they could hardly escape so utterly without religion.

But all must be used for some excellent purpose, wherefore they dissever and anatomize. . . . A superabundance of sense is necessary if anything is to escape this hostile treatment. On that account alone the number must be small who are capable of such a contemplation of any object as might awake in them religion.

But this development is still more checked. The utmost is done to divert the remaining sense from the Universe. Truth and all that in it is, must be confined in the limits of the civil life. All actions must bear upon this life, while, again, it is believed that the boasted inner harmony of man means that everything bears upon his actions and they never think that, if it is to be a true and free life, the existence of an individual in the state, even as of the state itself, must have arisen from the Whole. But they are sunk in blind idolatry of the existing civil life, they are convinced that it affords material enough for the sense and displays rich enough pictures. . . . The smallest thing that has influence in this sphere is not to be neglected, and the greatest, just because it goes further, is decried, as if it were mean and perverted. . . .

In the relations of man to this world there are certain openings into the Infinite, prospects past which all are led that their sense may find its way to the

Whole. Immediate feelings of definite content may not be produced by this glimpse, but there may be a general susceptibility to all religious feelings. Those prospects, therefore, are wisely blocked up, and in the opening some philosophical caricature is placed as an ill-favored place is at times covered by some sorry picture.

And if, as happens at times, the omnipotence of the Universe makes itself manifest in those people of understanding themselves, if some ray penetrating falls upon their eyes and their soul cannot be shielded from some stirring of those emotions, the Infinite is never a goal to which they fly for rest. It is as a post at the end of a course, simply a point to be rounded without touching at the greatest speed, and the sooner they can return to their old place the better.

Birth and death are such points. Before them it is impossible to forget that our own self is completely surrounded by the Infinite. Despite their frequency, so soon as they touch us more nearly, they always stir a quiet longing and a holy reverence. The measurelessness of sense perception is also a hint at least of a still higher infinity. But nothing would please better those persons of understanding than to be able to use the greatest radius of the system of the worlds, as men now use the meridian of the earth, for measuring and reckoning in common life. And, if the images of life and death do approach them, believe me, however much they may speak of religion, it does not lie so near their hearts as to use the occasion to win some few young people for caution and economy in the use of their powers and for the noble art of lengthening life.

Punished they certainly are. They reach no standpoint from which they might themselves rear, from the foundation, this worldly wisdom in which they trust, but move slavishly and reverently in ancient forms or divert themselves with little improvements. This is the extreme of utilitarianism to which the age with rapid strides is being hurried by worthless scholastic word-wisdom. This new barbarism is a fit counterpart of the old. . . .

Religion at present can only be advanced by the strongest resistance to this general tendency, and it cannot begin except by radical opposition. As everything follows the law of affinity, sense can only triumph by taking possession of an object on which this kind of understanding so hostile to it, hangs but loosely. This it will acquire most easily and with superfluity of free power. Now this object is the inner, not the outer world. . . . A religious man must be reflective, his sense must be occupied in the contemplation of himself. Being occupied with the profoundest depths, he abandons meanwhile all external things, intellectual as well as physical, leaving them to be the great aim of the researches of the people of understanding. In accordance with this law, the feeling for the Infinite is most readily developed in persons whose nature keeps them far from that which is the central point of all the opponents of the universal complete life. Hence it comes that, from of old, all truly religious characters have had a mystical trait, and that all imaginative natures, which are too airy to occupy themselves with solid and rigid worldly affairs, have at least some stirrings of piety. This is the character of all the religious appearances of our time; from those two colors, imagination and mysticism, though in various proportions, they are all composed. Appearances I say, because, in this state of things, more is scarcely to be expected.

Imaginative natures fail in penetrative spirit, in capacity for mastering the essential. A light changing play of beautiful, often charming, but merely fortuitous and entirely subjective combinations, satisfies them and is the highest they can conceive, and a deeper and inner connection presents itself in vain. . . . They have emotions of religion just as they have of art, philosophy and all things great and beautiful — they are attracted by the surface.

To the very nature of the other class, again, religion pre-eminently belongs. But their sense always remains turned towards themselves, for, in the present condition of the world, they do not know how to attain anything beyond, and they soon fail in material for cultivating their feeling to an independent piety. There is a great and powerful mysticism, not to be considered by the most frivolous man without reverence and devotion, which, by its heroic simplicity and proud scorn of the world, wrings admiration from the most judicious. It does not arise from being sated and overladen by external influences, but, on every occasion, some secret power ever drives the man back upon himself, and he finds himself to be the plan and key of the Whole. Convinced by a great analogy and a daring faith that it is not necessary to forsake himself, but that the spirit has enough in itself to be conscious of all that could be given from without, by a free resolve, he shuts his eyes for ever against all that is not himself. Yet this contempt is no ignorance, this closing of the sense no incapacity.

Thus, alas! it stands with our party at the present day. They have not learned to open their souls to Nature. Their living relation to it suffers from the clumsy way in which objects are rather indicated than shown, and they have neither sense nor light remaining from their self-contemplation sufficient to penetrate this ancient darkness. Wherefore, in scorn of this evil age, they would fain have nothing to do with its work in them. Their higher feeling is thus untrained and needy, and their true inward fellowship with the world is both confined and sickly. Alone with their sense, they are compelled to circulate eternally in an all too narrow sphere, and, after a sickly life, their religious sense dies, from want of attraction, of indirect weakness.

Another end awaits those whose sense for the highest turns boldly outwards, seeking there expansion and renovation for its life. Their disharmony with the age only too clearly appears, for they suffer a violent death, happy if you will, yet fearful, the suicide of the spirit. Not knowing how to comprehend the world, the essence and larger sense of which remains strange to them among the paltry views to which an outward constraint limits them, they are deceived by confused phenomena, abandoned to unbridled fancies, and seek the Universe and its traces where they never were. Finally they unwillingly rend asunder utterly the connection of the inner and the outer, chase the impotent understanding and end in a holy madness, the source of which almost no man knows. They are loud screaming but not understood victims of the general contempt and maltreatment of the heart of man. . . .

The strength and compass, as well as the purity

and clearness of every perception, depend upon the
keenness and vigor of the sense. Suppose the wisest
man without opened senses. He would not be nearer
religion than the most thoughtless and wanton who
only had an open and true sense. Here then we must
begin. An end must be made to the slavery in which
the sense of man is held, for the benefit of exercisings
of the understanding whereby nothing is exercised, of
those enlightenments that make nothing clear, of those
dissectings whereby nothing is resolved. This is an end
for which you will all labor with united powers. . . .
A juster idea of the sacredness of childhood and the
eternity of inviolable liberty is spreading. Even in the
first stages of development, it is seen that the manifestations of liberty must be expected and inquired for.
Soon those barriers shall be broken down; the intuitive
power will take possession of its whole domain, every
organ will be opened, and it will be possible for objects,
in all ways, to affect man.

With this regained liberty of sense, however, a
limitation and firm direction of the activity may very
well consist. This is the great demand from contemporaries and posterity, with which the best among you
are coming forward. You are tired of seeing barren,
encyclopedic versatility. Only by this way of self-
limitation have you become what you are, and you
know there is no other way to culture. You insist,
therefore, that everyone should seek to become something definite, and follow something with steadfastness
and concentration. No one can perceive the justice of
this counsel better than the man who has ripened to a
certain universality of sense, for he must know that,
except by separation and limitation, perception would

have no objects. I rejoice, therefore, at these efforts, and would they had had more success. Religion would thereby receive excellent help, for this very limitation of effort, if only the sense itself is not limited, all the more surely prepares for the sense the way to the Infinite and opens again the long interrupted intercourse. Whosoever has seen and known much and can then resolve, with his whole might, to do and forward something for its own sake, must recognize, if he is not to contradict himself, that other things have been made and have a right to existence for their own sakes. And when he has succeeded to the utmost in the object of his choice, it will least of all escape him at the summit of perfection that, without all the rest, this is nothing. This recognition of the strange and annihilation of the personal that urge themselves everywhere upon a thoughtful man, this seasonably changing love and contempt for all that is finite and limited are not possible without a dim presentiment of the World and God, and they must call forth a more definite longing for the One in the All.

Every man knows from his own consciousness three spheres of the sense in which its different manifestations are divided. First there is the interior of the Ego itself; second, the outer world, in so far as it is indefinite and incomplete — call it mass, matter, element, or what you will; the third seems to unite both, the sense turning, in constant change, within and without, and only finding peace in perceiving the absolute unity of both sides, which is the sphere of the individual, of what is complete in itself, of all that is art in nature, and in the works of man. Everyone is not equally at home in all those spheres, but from each there is a way to pious exaltations of the soul which take characteristic form simply according to the variety of the ways in which they have been found.

Study yourselves with unswerving attention, put aside all that is not self, proceed with the sense ever more closely directed to the purely inward. The more you pass by all foreign elements, making your personality appear diminished almost to the vanishing point, the clearer the Universe stands before you, and the more gloriously the terror of annihilating the fleeting is rewarded by the feeling of the eternal.

Look outside again on one of the widely distributed elements of the world. Seek to understand it in itself, and seek it in particular objects, in yourself and everywhere. Traverse again and again your way from center to circumference, going ever farther afield. You will rediscover everything everywhere, and you will only be able to recognize it in relation to its opposite. Soon everything individual and distinct will have been lost and the Universe be found.

What way now leads from the third sphere, from the sense for art? Its immediate object is by no means the Universe itself. It is an individual thing complete in itself and rounded off. There is satisfaction in each enjoyment, and the mind, peacefully sunk in it, is not driven to such a progress as would make the single thing gradually disappear and be replaced by the Universe. Is there nowhere any way, but must this sphere for ever remain apart, and artists be condemned to be irreligious? Or is there perhaps some other relation between art and religion? . . . If it is true that there are sudden conversions whereby in men, thinking of nothing less than of lifting themselves above the finite, in a moment, as by an immediate, inward illumination, the sense for the highest comes forth and surprises them by its splendor, I believe that more than anything else the sight of a great and sublime work of art can accomplish this miracle. And I would believe that, without any gradual approximation beforehand, you may perhaps be met by such a beam of your own sun and turned to religion.

By the first way of finding the Universe, the most abstracted self-contemplation, the most ancient eastern Mysticism, with marvelous boldness that resembled the more recent Idealism among us, linked the infinitely great to the infinitely little and found everything bordering on nothing.

From the contemplation of the masses and their counterparts, again, every religion, the pattern of which is the heavens or elemental nature, has manifestly proceeded. The polytheistic Egypt was long the most perfect nurse of this type of thought. In it we can at least guess that the purest intuition of the original and real may have walked in meek tolerance close beside the darkest superstitions and the most senseless mythology.

And if there is nothing to tell of a religion originating in art that has ruled peoples and times, it is all the clearer that the sense for art has never approached those two kinds of religion without covering them with new beauty and holiness and sweetly mitigating their original narrowness. Thus the ancient sages and poets, and above all, the artists of the Greeks, changed the natural religion into fairer, more gladsome form. In all the mythical representations of the divine Plato and his followers, which you would acknowledge rather as religious than as scientific, we perceive how beautifully that mystical self-contemplation mounts to the highest pinnacle of divineness and humanness. Simply by the ordinary life in the sphere of art and by a living endeavor, sustained by indwelling power and especially by poetic art, he penetrates from one form of religion to the opposite and unites both. One can only marvel, therefore, at the beautiful self-forgetfulness with which in holy zeal, as a just king that does not spare even his too soft-hearted mother, he speaks against art, for, where there was no corruption and no misunderstanding produced by corruption, the work of art was but a free-will service rendered to the imperfect natural religions. . . .

See then, whether you wish it or not, the goal of your highest endeavors is just the resurrection of religion. By your endeavors this event must be brought to pass, and I celebrate you as, however unintentionally, the rescuers and cherishers of religion. Do not abandon your post and your work till you have unlocked the recesses of knowledge, and, in priestlike humility, have opened the sanctuary of true science. Then all who draw nigh, and the sons of religion among them, will be compensated for what half knowledge and arrogance have made them lose.

Philosophy, exalting man to the consciousness of his reciprocity with the world, teaching him to know himself, not as a separate individual, but as a living, operative member of the Whole, will no longer endure to see the man who steadfastly turns his eye to his own spirit in search of the Universe, pine in poverty and need. The anxious wall of separation is broken down. The outer world is only another inner world.

Everything is the reflection of his own spirit, as his spirit is the copy of all things. He can seek himself in this reflection without losing himself or going outside of himself. He can never exhaust himself in contemplation of himself, for in himself everything lies.

Ethics, in its chaste and heavenly beauty, far from jealousy and despotic pride, will hand him at the entrance the heavenly lyre and the magic glass, that he may see in countless forms the earnest quiet image of the spirit ever the same and may accompany it with divine music.

Natural science sets the man who looks around him to discover the Universe, in the center of nature, and no longer suffers him to dissipate himself fruitlessly in the study of small details. He can now pursue the play of nature's powers into their most secret recesses, from the inaccessible storehouses of energized matter to the artistic workshops of the organic life. He measures its might from the bounds of world-filled space to the center of his own Ego, and finds himself everywhere in eternal strife and in closest union. He is nature's center and circumference. Delusion is gone and reality won. Sure is his glance and clear is his view. Under all disguises he detects it and nowhere rests except in the Infinite and the One. . . .

See how, without your aid, the heavenly growth flourishes in the midst of your plantings. It is a witness of the approval of the gods and of the imperishableness of your desert. Neither disturb it nor pluck it up; it is an ornament that adorns, a talisman that protects.

FOURTH SPEECH

Association in Religion, or Church and Priesthood

THOSE OF YOU who are accustomed to regard religion simply as a malady of the soul, usually cherish the idea that if the evil is not to be quite subdued, it is at least more endurable, so long as it only infects individuals here and there. On the other hand, the common danger is increased and everything put in jeopardy by too close association among the patients. So long as they are isolated, judicious treatment, due precautions against infection and a healthy spiritual atmosphere may allay the paroxysms and weaken, if they do not destroy, the virus, but in the other case the only remedy to be relied on is the curative influence of nature. The evil would be accompanied by the most dangerous symptoms and be far more deadly being nursed and heightened by the proximity of the infected. Even a few would then poison the whole atmosphere; the soundest bodies would be infected; all the canals in which the processes of life are carried on would be destroyed; all the juices would be decomposed; and, after undergoing such a feverish delirium, the healthy spiritual life and working of whole generations and peoples would be irrecoverably ruined. Hence your opposition to the church, to every institution meant for the communication of religion is always more violent than your opposition to religion itself, and priests, as the supports and specially active members of such institutions, are for you the most hated among men.

But those of you who have a somewhat milder view of religion, regarding it rather as an absurdity than as an absolute distraction, have an equally unfavorable idea of all organizations for fellowship. Slavish surrender of everything characteristic and free, spiritless mechanism and vain usages are, you consider, the inseparable consequences of every such institution. It is the skilful work of persons who with incredible success make great gain from things that are nothing, or which at least every other person could have done equally well. . . .

If there is religion at all, it must be social, for that is the nature of man, and it is quite peculiarly the nature of religion. You must confess that when an individual has produced and wrought out something in his own mind, it is morbid and in the highest degree unnatural to wish to reserve it to himself. He should express it in the indispensable fellowship and mutual dependence of action. And there is also a spiritual nature which he has in common with the rest of his species which demands that he express and communicate all that is in him. The more violently he is moved and the more deeply he is impressed, the stronger that social impulse works. And this is true even if we regard it only as the endeavor to find the feeling in others, and so to be sure that nothing has been encountered that is not human.

You see that this is not a case of endeavoring to

make others like ourselves, nor of believing that what
is in one man is indispensable for all. It is only the
endeavor to become conscious of and to exhibit the
true relation of our own life to the common nature
of man.

But indisputably the proper subjects for this
impulse to communicate are the conscious states and
feelings in which originally man feels himself passive.
He is urged on to learn whether it may not be an
alien and unworthy power that has produced them.
Those are the things which mankind from childhood
are chiefly engaged in communicating. His ideas,
about the origin of which he can have no doubts, he
would rather leave in quiet. Still more easily he re-
solves to reserve his judgments. But of all that enters
by the senses and stirs the feelings he will have wit-
nesses and participators. How could he keep to himself the most comprehensive and general influences
of the world when they appear to him the greatest
and most irresistible? How should he wish to reserve
what most strongly drives him out of himself and
makes him conscious that he cannot know himself
from himself alone? If a religious view become clear
to him, or a pious feeling stir his soul, it is rather his
first endeavor to direct others to the same subject and
if possible transmit the impulse.

The same nature that makes it necessary for the
pious person to speak, provides him also with an audi-
ence. No element of life, so much as religion, has
implanted along with it so vivid a feeling of man's
utter incapacity ever to exhaust it for himself alone.
No sooner has he any sense for it than he feels its
infinity and his own limits. He is conscious that he

grasps but a small part of it, and what he cannot himself reach he will, at least, so far as he is able, know and enjoy from the representations of those who have obtained it. This urges him to give his religion full expression, and seeking his own perfection, to listen to every note that he can recognize as religious. Thus mutual communication organizes itself, and speech and hearing are to all alike indispensable.

But the communication of religion is not like the communication of ideas and perceptions to be sought in books. In this medium, too much of the pure impression of the original production is lost. Like dark stuffs that absorb the greater part of the rays of light, so everything of the pious emotion that the inadequate signs do not embrace and give out again, is swallowed up. In the written communication of piety, everything needs to be twice or thrice repeated, the original medium requiring to be again exhibited, and still its effect on men in general in their great unity can only be badly copied by multiplied reflection. Only when it is chased from the society of the living, religion must hide its varied life in the dead letter.

Nor can this intercourse with the heart of man be carried on in common conversation. Many who have a regard for religion have upbraided our times, because our manners are such that in conversation in society and in friendly intercourse, we talk of all weighty subjects except of God and divine things. In our defense I would say, this is neither contempt nor indifference, but a very correct instinct. Where mirth and laughing dwell, and even earnestness must pliantly associate with joke and witticism, there can be no room for what must ever be attended by holy reserve and awe. Religious views, pious feelings, and earnest reflections, are not to be tossed from one to another in such small morsels as the materials of a light conversation. On sacred subjects it would be rather sacrilegious than fitting to be ready with an answer to every question and a response to every address. Religion, therefore, withdraws itself from too wide circles to the more familiar conversation of friendship or the dialogue of love, where glance and action are clearer than words, and where a solemn silence also is understood.

By way of the light and rapid exchange of retorts common in society divine things cannot be treated, but there must be a higher style and another kind of society entirely consecrated to religion. On the highest subject with which language has to deal, it is fitting that the fullness and splendor of human speech be expended. It is not as if there were any ornament that religion could not do without, but it would be impious and frivolous of its heralds, if they would not consecrate everything to it, if they would not collect all they possess that is glorious, that religion may, if possible, be presented in all power and dignity. Without poetic skill, therefore, religion can only be expressed and communicated rhetorically, in all power and skill of speech, and in its swiftness and inconstancy the service of every art that could aid, is willingly accepted. Hence a person whose heart is full of religion, only opens his mouth before an assembly where speech so richly equipped might have manifold working.

Would that I could depict to you the rich, the superabundant life in this city of God, when the

citizens assemble, each full of native force seeking
liberty of utterance and full at the same time of holy
desire to apprehend and appropriate what others offer.
When one stands out before the others he is neither
justified by office nor by compact; nor is it pride or
ignorance that inspires him with assurance. It is the
free impulse of his spirit, the feeling of heart-felt
unanimity and completest equality, the common abolition of all first and last, of all earthly order. He comes
forward to present to the sympathetic contemplation
of others his own heart as stirred by God, and, by
leading them into the region of religion where he is
at home, he would infect them with his own feeling.
He utters divine things and in solemn silence the congregation follow his inspired speech. If he unveils a
hidden wonder, or links with prophetic assurance the
future to the present, or by new examples confirms
old truths, or if his fiery imagination enchants him in
visions into another part of the world and into another order of things, the trained sense of the congregation accompanies him throughout. On returning
from his wanderings through the Kingdom of God
into himself, his heart and the hearts of all are but
the common seat of the same feeling. Let this harmony
of view announce itself, however softly, then there
are sacred mysteries discovered and solemnized that
are not mere insignificant emblems, but, rightly considered, are natural indications of a certain kind of
consciousness and certain feelings. It is like a loftier
choir that in its own noble tone answers the voice that
calls.

And this is not a mere simile, but, as such a
speech is music without song or melody, there may

be a music among the saints that is speech without words, giving most definite and comprehensible expression to the heart.

The muse of harmony, the intimate relation of which to religion has been long known, though acknowledged by few, has from of old laid on the altars of religion the most gorgeous and perfect works of her most devoted scholars. In sacred hymns and choruses to which the words of the poet are but loosely and airily appended, there are breathed out things that definite speech cannot grasp. The melodies of thought and feeling interchange and give mutual support, till all is satiated and full of the sacred and the infinite.

Of such a nature is the influence of religious men upon each other. Thus their natural and eternal union is produced. It is a heavenly bond, the most perfect production of the spiritual nature of man, not to be attained till man, in the highest sense, knows himself. Do not blame them if they value it more highly than the civil union which you place so far above all else, but which nevertheless will not ripen to manly beauty. Compared with that other union, it appears far more forced than free, far more transient than eternal.

But where, in all that I have said of the congregation of the pious, is that distinction between priests and laity to which you are accustomed to point as the source of so many evils? You have been deluded; this is no distinction of persons, but only of office and function. Every man is a priest, in so far as he draws others to himself in the field he has made his own and can show himself master in; every man is a layman, in so far as he follows the skill and direction of another in the religious matters with which he is less familiar. That tyrannical aristocracy which you describe as so hateful does not exist, but this society is a priestly nation, a complete republic, where each in turn is leader and people, following in others the same power that he feels in himself and uses for governing others.

How then can this be the home of the envy and strife that you consider the natural consequences of all religious associations? I see nothing but unity and, just by means of the social union of the pious, the gentle mingling of all the differences found in religion. . . . If unconstrained universality of the sense is the first and original condition of religion, and also, as is natural, its ripest fruit, you can surely see that, as religion advances and piety is purified, the whole religious world must appear as an indivisible whole.

The impulse to abstract, in so far as it proceeds to rigid separation, is a proof of imperfection. The highest and most cultured always see a universal union, and, in seeing it, establish it. Every man is only in contact with his neighbor; but on every side and in every direction he has neighbors and is thus inseparably bound up with the whole. Mystics and physicists in religion; those to whom the Deity is personal and those to whom He is not; those who have risen to a systematic view of the Universe, or those who only see it in its elements or as dim chaos should all be united. A band encloses them all and they cannot be quite separated, except forcibly and arbitrarily. Each separate association is a mobile, integrate part of the whole, losing itself in vague outlines in the whole, and it must ever be the better class of members who feel this truth. Whence then, if not from pure misunderstanding, is the wild mania for converting to single definite forms of religion that you denounce, and the awful watchword, "No salvation save with us"?

The society of the pious, as I have exhibited it and as from its nature it must be, is occupied purely with mutual communication, and subsists only among persons already having religion of some kind. How can it be their business to change the minds of those who already profess to have a definite religion, or to introduce and initiate persons who have none at all? The religion of this society as such is simply the collective religion of all the pious. As each one sees it in others it is infinite, and no single person can fully grasp it, for it is in no one instance a unity, not even when highest and most cultivated. If a man, therefore, has any share in religion, it matters not what, would it not be a mad proceeding for the society to rend from him that which suits his nature, for this element also it should embrace and therefore someone must possess it? And how would they cultivate persons to whom religion generally is still strange? Their heritage, the infinite Whole they cannot communicate to them, and any particular communication must proceed from an individual and not the society. Is there something general, indefinite, something common to all the members that a nonreligious person might receive? But you know that nothing in a general and indefinite form can actually be communicated. It must be individual and thoroughly definite, or it is nothing. This undertaking would have no measure and no rule. Besides, how would the society ever think of going beyond itself, seeing the need which gave it birth, the principle of religious association, has no such bearing? Individuals join and become a whole; the whole being satisfied with itself, abides in itself, and has no further endeavor.

Religious effort of this kind, therefore, is never more than a private business of individuals, and is, if I might so say, rather in so far as a man is outside the church than as he is within. When, impelled by sacred feelings, he must withdraw from the circle of religious association where the common existence and life in God affords the noblest enjoyment, into the lower regions of life, he can still bring all that there occupies him into relation with what to his spirit must ever remain the highest. On descending among persons limited to one earthly aim and effort, he is apt to believe—and let it be forgiven him—that, from intercourse with gods and muses, he has been transported among a race of rude barbarians. He feels himself a steward of religion among unbelievers, a missionary among savages. As an Orpheus or Amphion he hopes to win many by heavenly melody. He presents himself among them as a priestly figure, expressing clearly and vividly his higher sense in all his doings and in his whole nature. And if there be any response, how willingly he nurses those first presentiments of religion in a new soul, believing it to be a beautiful pledge of its growth, even under an alien and inclement sky, and how triumphantly he conducts the novice to the exalted assembly! This activity for the extension of religion is only the pious longing of the stranger for his home, the endeavor to carry his Fatherland with him, and find again everywhere its laws and customs which are his higher, more beauteous life. The Father-

land itself, blessed and complete in itself, knows no
such endeavor.

After all this, you will possibly say that I seem
to be quite at one with you. I have shown what the
church ought to be. Now, by not ascribing to the
ideal church any of the qualities which distinguish
the real, I have, almost as strongly as you, condemned
its present form. I assure you, however, I have not
spoken of what should be, but of what is, unless,
indeed, you deny the existence of what is only hin-
dered by the limits of space from appearing to the
coarser vision. The true church has, in fact, always
been thus, and still is, and if you cannot see it, the
blame is your own, and lies in a tolerably palpable
misunderstanding. Remember only—to use an old but
weighty expression—that I have not spoken of the
church militant, but of the church triumphant, not
of the church that fights against what the age and the
state of man place in its way, but of the church that
has vanquished all opposition, whose training is complete. I have exhibited a society of men who have
reached consciousness with their piety, and in whom
the religious view of life is dominant. As I trust I
have convinced you that they must be men of some
culture and much power, and that there can never
be but very few of them, you need not seek their
union where many hundreds, whose song strikes the
ear from afar, are assembled in great temples. So close
together, you well know, men of this kind do not
stand. Possibly anything of the sort collected in one
place is only to be found in single, separate communi-
ties, excluded from the great church. This at least
is certain, that all truly religious men, as many as

there have ever been, have not only had a belief, or
rather a living feeling of such a union, but have actually lived in it, and, at the same time, they have all
known how to estimate the church, commonly so-
called, at about its true value, which is to say, not particularly high.

The great association to which your strictures
properly apply, is very far from being a society of
religious men. It is only an association of persons who
are but seeking religion, and it seems to me natural
that, in almost every respect, it should be the counterpart of the true church. To make this as clear to
you as it is to myself, I must, alas! condescend upon
a mass of earthly and worldly things, and wind my
way through a labyrinth of marvelous confusions. It
is not done without repugnance, but it is necessary,
if you are to agree with me. Perhaps if I draw your
attention to the different forms of religious association
in the visible and in the true church, you will be convinced of my opinion in essentials. After what has
been said, you will, I hope, agree that in the true
religious society all communication is mutual. The
principle that urges us to give utterance to our own
experience, is closely connected with what draws us
to that which is strange, and thus action and reaction
are indivisibly united. Here, on the contrary, it is
quite different. All wish to receive, and there is only
one who ought to give. In entire passivity, they simply
suffer the impressions on their organs. So far as they
have power over themselves, they may aid in receiv-
ing, but of reaction on others they do not so much as
think. Does that not show clearly enough the difference in the principles of association? They can-

not be spoken of as wishing to complete their religion
through others, for if they had any religion of their
own, it would, from the necessity of its nature, show
itself in some way operative on others. They exercise
no reaction because they are capable of none; and they
can only be incapable because they have no religion.
Were I to use a figure from science—from which, in
matters of religion, I most willingly borrow expressions—I would say that they are negatively religious,
and press in great crowds to the few points where
they suspect the positive principle of religion. Having
been charged, however, they again fail in capacity
to retain. The emotion which could but play around
the surface very soon disappears. Then they go about
in a certain feeling of emptiness, till longing awakes
once more, and they gradually become again negatively electrified.

In few words, this is the history of their religious
life and the character of the social inclination that
runs through it. Not religion, but a little sense for
it, and a painful, lamentably fruitless endeavor to reach
it, are all that can be ascribed even to the best of
them, even to those who show both spirit and zeal.
In the course of their domestic and civil life, and
on the larger scene of which they are spectators, there
is much to stir persons with even a small share of
religious sense. But those emotions remain only a dim
presentiment, a weak impression on a soft mass, the
outlines of which at once become vague. Soon everything is swept away by the waves of the active life,
and is left stranded in the most unfrequented region
of the memory, where it will soon be entirely overlaid by worldly things.

From frequent repetition, however, of this little shock, a necessity at length arises. The dim something in the mind, always recurring, must finally be made clear. The best means, one would think, would be to take time to observe leisurely and attentively the cause. But it is not a single thing which they might abstract from all else, that works on them. It is all human things, and among them the different relations of their life in other departments. Then, from old habit, their sense will spontaneously turn to those relations and once more the sublime and infinite will, in their eyes, be broken up into single, miserable details. Feeling this, they do not trust themselves, but seek outside help. They would behold in the mirror of another person's representation that which in direct perception would soon dissolve.

In this way they seek to reach some higher, more defined consciousness, yet at the end they misunderstand this whole endeavor. If the utterances of a truly religious man awake all those memories, if they have received the combined impression of them, and go away deeply moved, they believe that their need is stilled, that the leading of their nature has been satisfied, and that they have in them the power and essence of all those feelings. Yet they have now as formerly, though it may be in a higher degree, but a fleeting, extraneous manifestation. Being without knowledge or guess of true religion, they remain subject to this delusion, and in the vain hope of at length attaining, they repeat a thousand times the same endeavor, and yet remain where and what they were.

If they advanced, and a spontaneous and living religion were implanted in them, they would soon not wish any more to be among those whose one-sidedness and passivity would no longer accord with their own state. They would at least seek beside them another sphere, where piety could show itself to others both living and life-giving, and soon they would wish to live altogether in it and devote to it their exclusive love. Thus in point of fact the church, as it exists among us, becomes of less consequence to men the more they increase in religion, and the most pious sever themselves coldly and proudly. Hardly anything could be clearer than that man is in this association merely because he is but seeking to be religious, and continues in it only so long as he has not yet attained. . . .

In comparison with the more glorious association which, in my view, is the only true church, I have spoken of this larger and widely extended association very disparagingly, as of something common and mean. This follows from the nature of the case, and I could not conceal my mind on the subject. I guard myself, however, most solemnly against any assumption you may cherish, that I agree with the growing wish that this institution should be utterly destroyed. Though the true church is always to stand open only to those who already have ripened to a piety of their own, there must be some bond of union with those who are still seeking. As that is what this institution should be, it ought, from the nature of the case, to take its leaders and priests always from the true church. Or is religion to be the single human concern in which there are to be no institutions for scholars and beginners? . . . .

I grant that in this society a disastrous sectarian

spirit exists and must exist. Where religious opinions are used as methods for attaining religion, they must, seeing a method requires to be thoroughly definite and finished, be formed into a definite whole. And where they are something that can only be given from without, being accepted on the authority of the giver, everyone whose religious speech is of a different cast, must be regarded as a disturber of quiet and sure progress, for by his very existence and the claims involved, he weakens this authority. Nay, I even grant that in the old Polytheism, where naturally religion could not be summed up as one, but willingly submitted to all division and severance, this sectarian spirit was much milder and more peaceable, and that in the otherwise better times of systematic religion it first organized itself and displayed its full power. Where all believe they have a complete system with a center, the value of details must be vastly greater.

I grant both; but you will admit that there is no reproach to religion in general, and there is no proof that the view of the Universe as system is not the highest stage of religion. I grant that in this society there is more regard to understanding and believing, to acting and to perfecting customs than is favorable to a free development of religious perceptions and feelings, and that in consequence, however enlightened its teaching be, it borders on some superstition and depends on some mythology; but you will admit, that, in that degree, its whole nature is distant from true religion. I grant that this association can hardly exist without a standing distinction between priests and laity as two different religious orders. Whosoever has cultivated in himself his feeling to dexterity in some kind of presentation, characteristically and completely, cannot possibly continue a layman, or conduct himself as if all this were wanting. He would be free, nay, bound, either to forsake this society and seek the true church, or to allow himself to be sent back by the true church to lead as a priest. This, however, remains certain, that this spirit of division with all that is unworthy in it and all its evil consequences, is not brought about by religion but by the want of religiousness in the multitude. . . .

Every fresh doctrine and revelation, every fresh view of the Universe that awakes the sense for it on some new side, may win some minds for religion who by no other way could be introduced into a higher world. To most of them naturally this particular aspect then remains for them the center of religion. They form around their master a school of their own, a self-existent, distinct part of the true and universal church which yet only ripens slowly and quietly towards union in spirit with the great whole. But before this is accomplished, as soon as the new feelings have permeated and satisfied all their soul, they are usually violently urged by the need to utter what is in them that they be not consumed of the fire within. Thus everyone proclaims the new salvation that has arisen for him. Every object suggests the newly discovered Infinite; every speech turns into a sketch of their peculiar religious views; every counsel, every wish, every friendly word is an inspired commendation of the sole way they know to salvation. Whosoever knows how religion operates, finds it natural that they all speak, for otherwise they would fear that the stones should surpass them. And whosoever knows how a new enthusiasm works, finds it natural that this living fire should kindle violently around, consume some and warm many, and give to thousands the surface imitation merely of a heart-felt glow.

And it is those thousands that work the mischief. The youthful zeal of the new saints accepts them as true brethren. What hinders, they say all too rashly, that these also should receive the Holy Ghost? Nay, they themselves believe that they have received, and, in joyous triumph, allow themselves to be conducted into the bosom of the pious society. But the intoxication of the first enthusiasm past, the glowing surface burnt out, they show themselves incapable of enduring and sharing the state allotted to the true believers. Compassionately the saints condescend to them, and, to go to their help, relinquish their own higher and deeper enjoyment. Thus everything takes that imperfect form. This comes to pass without outward causes through the corruption common to all human things. In accordance with that eternal order, the corruption most quickly seizes upon the most fiery and active life, that any section of the true church which might arise in isolation anywhere in the world, might not remain apart from all corruption, but be compelled to participate in it and form a false and degenerate church. In all times, among all peoples, in every religion this has happened.

Yet if things were only left quietly to themselves, this state could not anywhere long endure. Pour liquids of various gravities and densities, having small power of mutual attraction, into a vessel; shake them violently together till they seem to form one liquid, and you will see, if only you leave it quietly standing, how they will divide and only like associate itself to like. So would it have happened here, for it is the natural course of things. The true church would quietly have separated itself again to enjoy the higher, more intimate fellowship of which the rest are not capable. The bond among those that remained would then have been as good as loosed, and their natural dullness would then have had to look for something from without to determine what should become of them. And they would not have been forsaken by the members of the true church. Besides them, who would have had the smallest call to care for their state? What attraction would be offered to the regard of other men? What were to be won or what fame to be obtained from them?

The members of the true church could, therefore, have remained in undisturbed possession and might have entered upon their priestly office among them in a new and better appointed form. Every man would then have gathered around him those who best understood him, who by his method could be most strongly stirred. Instead of the vast association, the existence of which you now bewail, a great crowd of smaller, less definite societies would have arisen. In them men would in all kinds of ways, now here, now there, have tested religion. They would have been only states to be passed, preparatory for the time when the sense for religion should awake, and decisive for those who should be found incapable of being taken hold of in any way. . . .

As soon as a prince declared a church to be a community with special privileges, a distinguished member of the civil world, the corruption of that church was begun and almost irrevocably decided. And if the society of believing persons, and of persons desiring belief, had not been mixed after a wrong manner, that is always to the detriment of the former, this could not have happened, for otherwise no religious society could ever be large enough to draw the attention of the governor.

Such a constitutional act of political preponderance works on the religious society like the terrible head of Medusa. As soon as it appears everything turns to stone. Though without connection, everything that is for a moment combined, is now inseparably welded together; accidental elements that might easily have been ejected are now established for ever; drapery and body are made from one block and every unseemly fold is eternal. The greater and spurious society can no more be separated from the higher and smaller. It can neither be divided nor dissolved. It can neither alter its form nor its articles of faith. Its views and usages are all condemned to abide in their existing state.

But that is not all. The members of the true church the visible church may contain, are forcibly excluded from all share in its government, and are not in a position to do for it even the little that might still be done. There is more to govern than they either could or would do. There are worldly things now to order and manage, and privileges to maintain and make good. And even though in their domestic and civil affairs, they did know how to deal with such things, yet cannot they treat matters of this sort as a concern of their priestly office. That is an incongruity that their sense will not see into and to which

they cannot reconcile themselves. It does not accord
with their high and pure idea of religion and religious
fellowship. They cannot understand what they are
to make out of houses and lands and riches, either for
the true church to which they belong, or for the
larger society which they should conduct. By this
unnatural state of affairs the members of the true
church are distracted and perplexed.

But besides all this, persons are attracted who
otherwise would for ever have remained without.
If it is the interest of the proud, the ambitious, the
covetous, the intriguing to press into the church,
where otherwise they would have felt only the bit-
terest ennui, and if they begin to pretend interest and
intelligence in holy things to gain the earthly reward,
how can the truly religious escape subjection? And
who bears the blame if unworthy men replace ripe
saints, and if, under their supervision, everything
creeps in and establishes itself that is most contrary
to the spirit of religion? What but the state with its
ill-considered magnanimity?

But in a still more direct way, the state is the
cause why the bond between the true church and the
visible religious society has been loosened. After
showing to the church this fatal kindness, it believed
it had a right to its active gratitude, and transferred
to it three of its weightiest commissions. More or less
it has committed to the church the care and oversight
of education. Under the auspices of religion and in
the form of a congregation, it demands that the people
be instructed in those duties that cannot be set forth
in the form of law, that they be stirred up to a truly
citizenlike way of thinking, and that, by the power

of religion, they be made truthful in their utterances. As a recompense for those services, it robs it of its freedom, as is now to be seen in all parts of the civilized world where there is a state and a church. It treats the church as an institution of its own appointment and invention—and indeed its faults and abuses are almost all its own inventing; and it alone presumes to decide who is fit to come forward in this society as exemplar and as priest. And do you still charge it to religion that the visible church does not consist entirely of pious souls?

But I am not yet done with my indictment. The state pollutes religious fellowship by introducing into its deepest mysteries its own interests. When the church, in prophetic devoutness, consecrates the newborn babe to the Deity and to the struggle for the highest, the state will take the occasion to receive it from the hands of the church into the list of its *protégés*. When it gives the stripling its first kiss of brotherhood, as one who has taken his first glance into the sacred things of religion, this must also be for the state the evidence of the first stage of civil independence; if with pious wishes, it consecrates the union of two persons who, as emblems and instruments of creative nature, would at the same time consecrate themselves as bearers of the higher life, it must also be the state's sanction for the civil bond. The state will not even believe that a man has vanished from this earthly scene, till the church assures it that it has restored his soul to the Infinite and enclosed his dust in the sacred bosom of the earth. It shows reverence for religion and an endeavor to keep itself perpetually conscious of its own limits, that the state bows before religion and before its worshippers when it receives anything from the hands of the Infinite, or returns it again, but how all this works for the corruption of the religious society is clear enough. In all its regulations there is nothing directed to religion alone, nothing even in which religion is the chief matter. In the sacred speeches and instructions, as well as in the most mysterious and symbolical doings, everything has a legal and civil reference, everything is perverted from its original form and nature. Hence there are many among the leaders of the church who understand nothing of religion, but who yet, as servants of the state, are in a position to earn great official merit, and there are many among its members who do not even wish to seek religion, and who yet have interest enough to remain in the church and bear a part in it. . . .

This glance at the history of the ecclesiastical society is, I think, the best proof that it is not strictly a society of religious men. At most it appears that some particles of such a society are mixed in it and are overlaid with foreign ingredients. Before the first matter of this boundless corruption could have been admitted, the whole must have been in a state of morbid fermentation in which the few sound portions soon utterly disappeared.

Full of sacred pride, the true church would have refused gifts it could not use, well knowing that those who have found the Deity and have a common joy in knowing Him, have in the pure fellowship in which alone they would exhibit and communicate their utmost nature, really nothing in common the possession of which could be protected by worldly power. On earth they require nothing but a speech by which to make themselves understood and a space in which to be together, things requiring no prince's favor. . . . Away then with every such union between church and state! That remains my Cato's utterance to the end, or till I see the union actually destroyed.

Away too with all that has even a semblance to rigid union of priest and laity, whether among themselves or with each other! Learners shall not form bodies, for, even in mechanical trades, it can be seen how little that profits. And the priests, I mean as such, shall form no brotherhood among themselves. They shall neither divide their work nor their knowledge according to corporations, but let each man do his own duty without concerning himself about others, or having in this matter closer connection with one than with another. Between teacher and congregation also, there shall be no firm outward bond. According to the principles of the true church, the mission of a priest in the world is a private business, and the temple should also be a private chamber where he lifts up his voice to give utterance to religion. Let there be an assembly before him and not a congregation. Let him be a speaker for all who will hear, but not a shepherd for a definite flock. . . .

The visible religious society can only be brought nearer the universal freedom and majestic unity of the true church by becoming a mobile mass, having no distinct outlines, but each part being now here, now there, and all peacefully mingling together. The hateful sectarian and proselytizing spirit which leads ever farther astray from the essentials of religion, can only be extinguished when no one, any more, is informed that he belongs to a distinct circle, and is for other circles of a different faith. . . . But till something of this kind does happen, a heavy fate must lie upon all holy souls, who, glowing with religion, would seek to exhibit their most holy things even in the profane world, that something might thereby be accomplished. . . .

But this cannot be taken from them, that they can proclaim by a priestlike life the spirit of religion, and this may be their consolation and their best reward. In a holy person everything is significant; in an acknowledged priest of religion everything has a canonical meaning. They may, therefore, in all their movements exhibit the nature of religion. Even in the common relations of life nothing may be lost of the expression of a pious mind. The holy ardor with which they treat everything shows that even in trifles that a profane spirit skims over thoughtlessly, the music of noble feelings resounds in them. The majestic calm with which they equalize small and great, shows that they refer everything to the Unchangeable and in all things alike perceive the Deity. The bright serenity with which they pass every trace of decay, reveals to all how they live above time and above the world. The utmost ease of self-denial indicates how much of the limits of personality they have already abolished. The constantly open and active sense that neither the rarest nor the commonest escapes, shows how unweariedly they seek the Deity and listen for His voice. If in this way the whole life and every movement of soul and body is a priestlike work of art, the sense for what dwells in them may by this dumb speech be awakened in many.

And not content to express the nature of religion, they must also in a similar way destroy the false appearance of it. With childlike ingenuousness, and in the high simplicity of utter unconsciousness, seeing no danger, and feeling no need of courage, they disregard what base prejudices and subtle superstition have surrounded with a spurious glory of sanctity. Unconcerned as the infant Hercules, they let themselves be hissed at from all quarters by the snakes of solemn calumny, being able to crush them quietly in a moment. To this holy service they may devote themselves till better times, and I think that you also will have reverence for this unassuming worth, and will augur well for its influence on men.

But what am I to say to those to whom you refuse the priestly robe because they have not gone through a definite course of science in a definite way? Whither shall I direct them with the social bent of their religion not directed alone to the true church, but also outward to the world? Having no greater scene in which, in any striking way, they might appear, they may rest satisfied with the priestly service of their household gods. One family can be the most cultured element and the truest picture of the Universe. When quietly and securely all things work together, all the powers that animate the Infinite are thus operative; when all advances in quiet joyousness, the high World-Spirit rules in it; when the music of love accompanies all movements, the harmony of the spheres resounds, resounds in the smallest space. They may construct this sanctuary, order it and cherish it. In pious might they may set it up clearly and evidently; with love and spirit they may dispose it. By this means many will learn to contemplate the Universe in the small, obscure dwelling. It will be a Holy of Holies in which many will receive the consecration of religion. This priesthood was the first in the holy and infant world, and it will be the last when no other is any longer necessary.

Nay, at the end of our future culture we expect a time when no other society preparatory for religion except the pious family life will be required. At present, millions of men and women of all ranks sigh under a load of mechanical and unworthy labors. The older generation succumbs discouraged, and, with pardonable inertness, abandons the younger generation to accident in almost everything, except the necessity straightway to imitate and learn the same degradation. That is the cause why the youth of the people do not acquire the free and open glance whereby alone the object of piety is found. There is no greater hindrance to religion than that we must be our own slaves, and everyone is a slave who must execute something it ought to be possible to do by dead force. We hope that by the perfecting of sciences and arts, those dead forces will be made serviceable to us, and the corporeal world, and everything of the spiritual that can be regulated, be turned into an enchanted castle where the god of the earth only needs to utter a magic word or press a spring, and what he requires will be done. Then for the first time, every man will be free-born; then every life will be at once practical and contemplative; the lash of the task-master will be lifted over no man; and everyone will have peace and leisure for contemplating the world in himself. It is only the unfortunate to whom this is wanting, from whose spiritual organs all nourishing forces are withdrawn because their whole being must be spent untiringly in mechanical service, that need individual, fortunate souls to come forward and assemble them about them, to be their eye for them, and in a few swift minutes communicate to them the highest content of a life. But when the happy time comes and everyone can freely exercise and use his sense, at the very first awaking of the higher powers, in sacred youth, under the care of paternal wisdom, all who are capable will participate in religion. All communication that is not mutual will then cease, and the father, well repaid, will lead the stout son, not only into a more joyful world and a lighter life, but straightway into the sacred assembly also of the worshippers of the Eternal, now increased in number and activity.

In the grateful feeling that, when this better time has come, however far off it may still be, the efforts to which you have devoted your days shall have contributed somewhat to its coming, permit me once more to direct your attention to the fair fruit of your labor. Allow yourselves to be led once more to the exalted fellowship of truly religious souls. It is dispersed and almost invisible, but its spirit rules everywhere, even where but few are gathered in the name of the Deity. What is there in it that should not fill you with admiration and esteem, ye friends and admirers of the good and beautiful? They are among themselves an academy of priests. The exhibition of the holy life, which for them is the highest, is treated by everyone as his art and study, and the Deity out of His endless riches apportions to each one his own lot. To a universal sense for everything belonging to the sacred sphere of religion, every man joins as artists should, the endeavor to perfect himself in some one department. A noble rivalry prevails, and a longing to produce something worthy of such an assembly makes everyone with faithfulness and diligence master all that belongs to his special section. In a pure heart it is preserved, with concentrated mind it is arranged, by heavenly art it is molded and perfected. Thus in every way and from every source, acknowledgment and praise of the Infinite resound, everyone bringing, with joyous heart, the ripest fruit of his thinking and examining, of his comprehending and feeling. They are also among themselves a choir of friends. Everyone knows that he is both a part and a work of the Universe, in him also its divine life and working being revealed. He, therefore, regards himself as an object worthy of the attention of others. With sacred reserve, yet with a ready openness that all may enter and behold, he lays bare everything of the relations of the Universe of which he is conscious and what of the elements of humanity takes individual shape in him. Why should they hide anything from one another? All that is human is holy, for all is divine. Again, they are among themselves a band of brothers — or have you perhaps an intenser expression for the entire blending of their natures, not in respect of existence and working, but in respect of sense and understanding? The more everyone approaches the Universe and the more they communicate to one another, the more perfectly they all become one. No one has a consciousness for himself, each has also that of his neighbor. They are no longer men, but mankind also. Going out of themselves and triumphing over themselves, they are on the way to true immortality and eternity.

If in any other department of life, or in any other school of wisdom, you have found anything nobler than this, impart it to me; mine I have given you.

FIFTH SPEECH

The Religions

MAN IN CLOSEST FELLOWSHIP with the highest must be for you all an object of esteem, nay, of reverence. No one capable of understanding such a state can, when he sees it, withhold this feeling. That is past all doubt. You may despise all whose minds are easily and entirely filled with trivial things, but in vain you attempt to depreciate one who drinks in the greatest for his nourishment. You may love him or hate him, according as he goes with you or against you in the narrow path of activity and culture, but even the most beautiful feeling of equality you cannot entertain towards a person so far exalted above you. The seeker for the Highest Existence in the world stands above all who have not a like purpose. Your wisest men say that, even against your will, you must honor the virtuous who, in accordance with the laws of the moral nature, endeavor to determine finite concerns by infinite requirements. And were it even possible for you to find something ridiculous in virtue itself, because of the contrast between the limited powers and the infinite undertaking, you still could not deny esteem to one whose organs are open to the Universe, who is far from strife and opposition, exalted above all imperfect endeavor, responsive to the Universe and one with it. You cannot despise when you see man in this supreme moment of human existence and the clear beam is reflected in its purity upon you.

But whether the picture of the nature and of the life of religion I have drawn has claimed your esteem I do not inquire. Because of false conceptions and devotion to non-essentials esteem is too often refused, but I am sure of the power of the subject, as soon as it is freed from its distorting drapery. Nor do I ask whether my thoughts on the coherence of this indwelling capacity with all that is sublime and godlike in our nature, have stimulated you to an intenser study of our nature and possibilities. I also pass the question, whether you have taken the higher standpoint I showed you, and have recognized from thence, in that nobler fellowship of spirits, so much misjudged, wherein everyone freely surrenders himself, not regarding the glory of his self-will, nor the exclusive possession of his deepest, most secret individuality, that he may regard himself as a work of the eternal, the all-fashioning World-Spirit, even the holy of holies of fellowship, higher far than the tenderest tie of friendship. In short, I do not ask whether all religion, in its infinity, its divine power, has compelled you to adoration, for I leave the matter itself to work upon you.

At present I have something else to deal with, a new opposition to vanquish. I would, as it were, conduct you to the God that has become flesh; I would show you religion when it has resigned its infinity and appeared, often in sorry form, among men; I would have you discover religion in the religions. Though they are always earthly and impure, the same form of heavenly beauty that I have tried to depict is to be sought in them.

The divisions of the church and the difference of religion are almost always found together. The connection seems inseparable. There are as many creeds and confessions as churches and religious communions. Glancing at this state of things, you might easily believe that my judgment on the plurality of the church must also be my judgment on the plurality of religion. You would, however, entirely mistake my opinion. I condemned the plurality of the church, but my argument presupposed the plurality of religion. I showed from the nature of the case that in the church all rigid outline should be lost, that all distinct partition should disappear. Not only did I hold that all should be one indivisible whole in spirit and sympathy, but that the actual connection should have larger development and ever approach the highest, the universal unity. Now if there is not everywhere plurality of religion, if the most marked difference is not necessary and unavoidable, why should the true church need to be one? Is it not that everyone in the religion of others may see and share what he cannot find in his own? And why should the visible church be only one, if it is not that everyone may seek in it religion in the form best fitted to awake the germ that lies asleep in him? And if this germ can only be fertilized and made to grow by one definite kind of influence, it must itself be of a definite kind.

Nor can these different manifestations of religion be mere component parts, differing only in number and size, and forming, when combined, a uniform whole. In that case every one would by natural progress come to be like his neighbor. Such religion as he acquired would change into his own, and become identical with it. The church, this fellowship with all believers which I consider indispensable for every religious man, would be merely provisional. The more successful its work, the quicker would it end—a view of the institution I have never contemplated. I therefore find that multiplicity of the religions is based in the nature of religion.

That no man can perfectly possess all religion is easy to see. Men are determined in one special way, religion is endlessly determinable. But it must be equally evident that religion is not dismembered and scattered in parts at random among men, but that it must organize itself in manifestations of varying degrees of resemblance. . . . This multiplicity is necessary for the complete manifestation of religion. It must seek for a definite character, not only in the individual but also in the society. Did the society not contain a principle to individualize itself, it could have no existence. Hence we must assume and we must search for an endless mass of distinct forms. Each separate religion claims to be such a distinct form revealing religion, and we must see whether it is agreeable to this principle. We must make clear to ourselves wherein it is peculiar. Though the difference be hidden under strange disguises, though it be distorted, not only by the unavoidable influence of the transitory to which the enduring has condescended, but also by the unholy hand of sacrilegious men, we must find it.

To be satisfied with a mere general idea of religion would not be worthy of you. Would you then understand it as it really exists and displays itself, would you comprehend it as an endlessly progressive work of the Spirit that reveals Himself in all human history, you must abandon the vain and foolish wish that there should only be one religion; you must lay aside all repugnance to its multiplicity; as candidly as possible you must approach everything that has ever, in the changing shapes of humanity, been developed in its advancing career, from the ever fruitful bosom of the spiritual life.

The different existing manifestations of religion you call positive religions. Under this name they have long been the object of a quite pre-eminent hate. Despite your repugnance to religion generally, you have always borne more easily with what for distinction is called natural religion. You have almost spoken of it with esteem.

I do not hesitate to say at once that from the heart I entirely deny this superiority. For all who have religion at all and profess to love it, it would be the vilest inconsequence to admit it. They would thereby fall into the openest self-contradiction. For my own part, if I only succeeded in recommending to you this natural religion, I would consider that I had lost my pains.

For you, indeed, to whom religion generally is offensive, I have always considered this preference natural. The so-called natural religion is usually so much refined away, and has such metaphysical and moral graces, that little of the peculiar character of religion appears. It understands so well to live in reserve, to restrain and to accommodate itself that it can be put up with anywhere. Every positive religion, on the contrary, has certain strong traits and a very marked physiognomy, so that its every moment, even to the careless glance, proclaims what it really is. . . .

But you may not admit this argument. You may transfer all the reproaches you have formerly been accustomed to bestow on religion in general to the single religions. You may maintain that there are always, just in this element that you call positive, the occasion and the justification of those reproaches, and that in consequence the positive religions cannot be as I have sought to represent, the natural manifestations of the true religion. You would show me how, without exception, they are full of what, according to my own statement, is not religion. Consequently, must not a principle of corruption lie deep in their constitution? You will remind me that each one proclaims that it alone is true, and that what is peculiar to it is absolutely the highest. Are they not distinguished from one another by elements they should as much as possible eliminate? In disproving and contending, be it with art and understanding, or with weapons stranger and more unworthy, do they not show themselves quite contrary to the nature of true religion? You would add that, exactly in proportion as you esteem religion and acknowledge its importance, you must take a lively interest in seeing that it everywhere enjoys the greatest freedom to cultivate itself on all sides. You must, therefore, hate keenly those definite religious forms, that hold all their adherents to the same type and the same word, withdraw the freedom to follow their own nature and compress them in un-

natural limits. In contrast, you would praise mightily
the superiority in all these points of the natural to
the positive religions.

Once more I say, I do not deny that misunderstandings and perversions exist in all religions, and
I raise no objections to the dislike with which they
inspire you. Nay, I acknowledge there is in them all
this much bewailed degeneration, this divergence into
alien territory. The diviner religion itself is, the less
would I embellish its corruptions, or admiringly cherish its excrescences. But forget for once this one-sided
view and follow me to another. Consider how much
of this corruption is due to those who have dragged
forth religion from the depths of the heart into the
civil world. Acknowledge that much of it is unavoidable as soon as the Infinite, by descending into the
sphere of time and submitting to the general influences
of finite things, takes to itself a narrow shell. And
however deep-rooted this corruption may be, and
however much the religions may have suffered thereby, consider this also: if the proper religious view of
all things is to seek even in things apparently common
and base every trace of the divine, the true and the
eternal, and to reverence even the faintest, you cannot omit what has the justest claims to be judged
religiously.

And you would find more than remote traces of
the Deity. I invite you to study every faith professed
by man, every religion that has a name and a character.
Though it may long ago have degenerated into a long
series of empty customs, into a system of abstract ideas
and theories, will you not, when you examine the
original elements at the source, find that this dead

dross was once the molten outpourings of the inner fire? Is there not in all religions more or less of the true nature of religion, as I have presented it to you? Must not, therefore, each religion be one of the special forms which mankind, in some region of the earth and at some stage of development, has to accept? . . .

The positive religions are just the definite forms in which religion must exhibit itself—a thing to which your so-called natural religions have no claim. They are only a vague, sorry, poor thought that corresponds to no reality, and you will find that in the positive religions alone a true individual cultivation of the religious capacity is possible. Nor do they, by their nature, injure the freedom of their adherents.

Why have I assumed that religion can only be given fully in a great multitude of forms of the utmost definiteness? Only on grounds that naturally follow from what has been said of the nature of religion. The whole of religion is nothing but the sum of all relations of man to God, apprehended in all the possible ways in which any man can be immediately conscious in his life. In this sense there is but one religion, for it would be but a poverty-stricken and halting life, if all these relations did not exist wherever religion ought to be. Yet all men will not by any means apprehend them in the same way, but quite differently. Now this difference alone is felt and alone can be exhibited while the reduction of all differences is only thought.

You are wrong, therefore, with your universal religion that is natural to all, for no one will have his own true and right religion, if it is the same for all. As long as we occupy a place there must be in these relations of man to the whole a nearer and a farther, which will necessarily determine each feeling differently in each life. Again, as long as we are individuals, every man has greater receptiveness for some religious experiences and feelings than for others. In this way everything is different. Manifestly then, no single relation can accord to every feeling its due. It requires the sum of them. Hence, the whole of religion can be present only, when all those different views of every relation are actually given. This is not possible except in an endless number of different forms. They must be determined adequately by a different principle of reference to the others, and in each the same religious element must be characteristically modified. In short, they must be true individuals. . . .

The whole of religion can only be actually given in the sum of all the forms possible in this sense. It can, therefore, be exhibited only in an endless series of shapes that are gradually developed in different points of time and space, and nothing adds to its complete manifestation that is not found in one of those forms. Where religion is so molded that everything is seen and felt in connection with one relation to the Deity that mediates it or embraces it, it matters not in what place or in what man it is formed or what relation is selected, it is a strictly positive religion. In respect of the sum of the religious elements—to use a word that should again be brought to honor—it is a heresy, for from many equals one is chosen to be head of the rest. In respect, however, of the fellowship of all participants and their relation to the founder of their religion who first raised this central point to clear consciousness, it is a school and a discipleship.

But if, as is to be hoped, we are agreed that religion can only be exhibited in and by such definite forms, only those who with their own religion pitch their camp in some such positive form, have any fixed abode, and, if I might so say, any well-earned right of citizenship in the religious world. They alone can boast of contributing to the existence and the progress of the whole, and they alone are in the full sense religious persons, on one side belonging by community of type to a kindred, on the other being distinguished by persistent and definite traits from everyone else.

But many perhaps who take an interest in the affairs of religion may ask with consternation, or some evil-disposed person may ask with guile, whether every pious person must connect himself with one of the existing forms of religion. Provisionally, I would say, by no means. It is only necessary that his religion be developed in himself characteristically and definitely. That it should resemble any great, largely accepted, existing form is not equally necessary. I would remind him that I have never spoken of two or three definite forms, and said that they are to be the only ones. Rather, they may ever more develop in countless numbers from all points. Whosoever does not find himself at home in an existing religion, I might almost say whosoever is not in a position to make it if he had not found it, must belong to none but should be held bound to produce a new one for himself. Is he alone in it and without disciples, it does not matter. Everywhere there are germs that cannot arrive at any more extended existence, and the religion of one person may have a definite form and organization, and be quite as genuinely a positive religion as if he had founded the greatest school.

In my opinion, then, you will see that the existing forms should not in themselves hinder any man from developing a religion suitable to his own nature and his own religious sense. The question of abiding in one of them or of constructing a religion of one's own, depends entirely on what relation develops in a man as fundamental feeling and middle point of all religions.

This is my provisional answer, but if he will hear more I would add that, except by misunderstanding, it would be very difficult to find oneself in such a position. A new revelation is never trivial, and merely personal, but always rests on something great and common. Hence adherents and fellow-believers have never failed the man really called to institute a new religion. Most men, following their nature, will belong to an existing form, and there will be only few whom none suffices.

Yet—and this is my chief point—the authority being the same for all, the many are no less free than the few, and do no less fashion something of their own. If we follow any man's religious history, we find first dim presentiments which never quite stir the depths of the heart, and, being unrecognized, again disappear. Around every man, especially in earlier days, they doubtless hover. Some hint may awaken them, and they may again vanish without reaching any definite form and betraying aught characteristic. Afterwards it first comes to pass that the sense for the Universe rises once for all into clear consciousness. One man discovers it in one relation, another in an-

other. Hereafter all things are referred to this relation, and so group themselves around it. Such a moment, therefore, in the strictest sense, determines every man's religion. Now I hope you will not consider a man's religion less characteristic, less his own, because it lies in a region where already several are collected. In this similarity you are not to find a mechanical influence of custom or birth, but, as you do in other cases, you are to recognize a common determination by higher causes. This agreement is a guarantee of naturalness and truth, and cannot, whether one is first or last, be hurtful to individuality. Though thousands before him and after him referred their religious life to one relation, would it, therefore, be the same in all?

Remember that every definite form of religion is exhaustless for any one man. In its own way it should embrace the whole, a thing too great for any man. And not only so, but in itself there exist endless varieties of cultivation which are, as it were, subordinate types of religion. Is there not here work and scope enough for all? I, at least, am not aware that any religion had succeeded in so taking possession of its territory, and had so determined and exhibited everything therein, according to its own spirit, that, in any one professor of distinguished gifts and individuality of mind, nothing is wanting to perfection. Only to few of our historical religions has it been granted, even in the time of their freedom and higher life, to develop rightly and perfectly the neighborhood of the middle point, and, in even a few forms, to give individual impress to the common character. The harvest is great but the laborers are few. An infinite field is opened in each of those religions, wherein thousands may scatter themselves. Uncultivated regions enough present themselves to every one who is capable of making and producing something of his own.

The charge that everyone who allows himself to be embraced in a positive religion, can only be an imitator of those who have given it currency and cannot develop himself individually, is baseless. This judgment no more applies here, than it would to the state or to society. It seems to us morbid or quixotic for any one to maintain that he has no room in any existing institution, and that he must exclude himself from society. We are convinced that every healthy person will, in common with many, have a great national character. Just because he is rooted in it and influenced by it, he can develop his individuality with the greatest precision and beauty. Similarly, in religion only morbid aberration so cuts off a man from a life in fellowship with those among whom nature has placed him, that he belongs to no great whole. Somewhere, on a great scale, everyone will find exhibited or will himself exhibit what for him is the middle point of religion. To every such common sphere we ascribe a boundless activity that goes into detail, in virtue of which all individual characteristics issue from its bosom. Thus understood, the church is with right called the common mother of us all.

To take the nearest example, think of Christianity as a definite individual form of the highest order. First there is in our time the well known outward division, so definite and pronounced. Under each section there is then a mass of different views and schools. Each exhibits a characteristic development, and has a founder and adherents, yet the last and most personal development of religiousness remains for each individual, and so much is it one with his nature that no one can fully acquire it but himself. And the more a man, by his whole nature, has a claim to belong to you, ye cultured, the more religion must reach this stage in him, for his higher feeling, gradually developing and uniting with other educated capacities, must be a characteristic product. . . .

In that moment in which in any man a definite consciousness of his relation to the highest Being has, as it were, original birth, an individual religious life originates. It is individual, not by an irreversible limitation to a particular number and selection of feelings and intuitions, not by the quality of the religious matter. This matter all who have the spiritual birth at the same time and in the same religious surroundings have in common. But it is individual by what he can have in common with no man, by the abiding influence of the peculiar circumstances in which his spirit was first greeted and embraced by the Universe, and by the peculiar way in which he conducts his observation and reflection on the same. This character and tone of the first childhood of his religion are borne by the whole subsequent course of his views and feelings, and are never lost, however far he may advance in fellowship with the Eternal Fountainhead. . . .

Thus you can only understand the religious person in so far as you know how to discover the whole in the notable moment that began his higher life, or from the developed manifestation can trace back this uniform character to the first, dimmest times of life. . . .

Resistance to the positive and arbitrary is resistance to the definite and real. If a definite religion may not begin with an original fact, it cannot begin at all. There must be a common ground for selecting some one religious element and placing it at the center, and this ground can only be a fact. And if a religion is not to be definite it is not a religion at all, for religion is not a name to be applied to loose, unconnected impulses. Recall what the poet says of a state of souls before birth. Suppose someone were to object to come into the world because he would not be this man or that, but a man in general! The polemic of natural religion against the positive is this polemic against life and it is the permanent state of its adherents.

Go back then, if you are in earnest about beholding religion in its definiteness, from this enlightened natural religion to those despised positive religions. There everything appears active, strong and secure, every single intuition has its definite content and its own relation to the rest, and every feeling has its proper sphere and its peculiar reference. You find somewhere every modification of religiousness and every mental state in which religion can place men, with each of its effects somewhere complete. Common institutions and single utterances alike testify that religion is valued almost to forgetfulness of all else. The holy zeal with which it is contemplated, communicated and enjoyed, and the child-like longing with which new revelations of heavenly power are expected, guarantee that no element visible from this standpoint shall be overlooked, and that nothing has disappeared without leaving a monument. Consider the variety of forms in which every single kind of fellowship with the Universe has already appeared. Do not be scared either by mysterious darkness or by wonderful dazzling grotesque traits. Do not admit the delusion that it may all be imagination and romance. Dig ever deeper where your magic rod has once pointed, and without fail you will bring forth the heavenly stream to the light of day.

But regard also the human which is to receive the divine. Do not forget that religion bears traces of the culture of every age and of the history of every race of men. Often it must go about in the form of a servant, displaying in its surroundings and in its adorning the poverty of its home and its disciples. You must not overlook how it has often been stunted in its growth from want of room to exercise its powers, and how from childhood it has pined miserably from bad treatment and ill-chosen nourishment.

And if you would comprehend the whole, do not abide by the various forms of religion that for centuries have shone and have dominated great peoples, and have been glorified in many ways by poets and sages. Recollect that what is historically and religiously most noteworthy is often distributed among but few, and remains hidden to the common eye. . . .

Religious men are throughout historical. That is not their smallest praise, but it is also the source of great misunderstandings. The moment when they were first filled with that consciousness which they have made the center of their religion is always sacred for them. Without reference to it, they never speak of what for them is characteristic in religion and of the form to which in themselves it has attained. You can easily imagine, then, how much more sacred still the moment must be in which this infinite intuition was first of all set up in the world as the foundation and center of one peculiar religion. To it the whole development of this religion in all generations and individuals is historically linked. Now this sum of the religion, and the religious culture of a great body of mankind, is something infinitely greater than a man's own religious life, and the little mirror of this religion which he personally exhibits. This fact then is glorified in all ways; every ornament of religious art is heaped upon it. It is worshiped as the greatest and most blessed miracle of the Highest. Men never speak of their religion, nor ever exhibit any of its elements except in connection with this fact.

As a consequence nothing is more natural than that this fact should be confused with the fundamental intuition of the religion. This has misled almost everyone and distorted the view of almost all religions. Never forget that the fundamental intuition of a religion must be some intuition of the Infinite in the finite, some one universal religious relation, found in every other religion that would be complete, but in this one only placed in the center. . . .

Above all I beg you not to be misled by the two hostile principles that everywhere, and almost from the earliest times, have sought to distort and obscure the spirit of religion. Some would circumscribe it to a single dogma, and exclude everything not fashioned in agreement with it, others, from hatred to polemics, or to make religion more agreeable to the irreligious, or from misunderstanding and ignorance of the matter, or from lack of religious sense, decry everything characteristic as dead letter. Guard yourselves from both. With rigid systematizers or shallow indifferentists you will not find the spirit of a religion. It is found only among those who live in it as their element, and ever advance in it without cherishing the folly that they embrace it all.

Whether with these precautions you will succeed in discovering the spirit of the religions I do not know. I fear religion is only comprehensible through itself, and that its special architecture and characteristic difference will not become clear till you yourselves belong to some one religion.

How you may succeed in deciphering the rude and undeveloped religions of remote peoples, or in unraveling the manifold, varied religious phenomena lying wrapped up in the beautiful mythologies of Greece and Rome, I care very little. May your gods guide you! But when you approach the holiest in which the Universe in its highest unity and comprehensiveness is to be perceived, when you would contemplate the different forms of the highest stage of religion which is not foreign or strange, but more or less existent among ourselves, I cannot be indifferent as to whether or not you find the right point of view. . . .

The original intuition of Christianity is more glorious, more sublime, more worthy of adult humanity, penetrates deeper into the spirit of systematic religion and extends itself further over the whole Universe. It is just the intuition of the Universal resistance of finite things to the unity of the Whole, and of the way the Deity treats this resistance. Christianity sees how He reconciles the hostility to Himself, and sets bounds to the ever-increasing alienation by scattering points here and there over the whole that are at once finite and infinite, human and divine. Corruption and redemption, hostility and mediation, are the two indivisibly united, fundamental elements of this type of feeling, and by them the whole form of Christianity and the cast of all the religious matter contained in it are determined. With ever-increasing speed the spiritual world has departed from its perfection and imperishable beauty. All evil, even this that the finite must decay before it has completed the circuit of its existence, is a consequence of the will, of the self-seeking endeavor of the isolated nature that, everywhere rending itself from its connection with the Whole, seeks to be something by itself. Death itself has come on account of sin. The spiritual world, going from bad to worse, is incapable of any production in which the Divine Spirit actually lives. The understanding being darkened has swerved from the truth; the heart is corrupt and has no praise before God; the image of the Infinite in every part of finite nature has gone extinct.

In accordance with this state of the spiritual world, all dealings of Divine Providence are calculated. They are never directed to the immediate results for feeling; they do not consider the happiness or suffering which they produce; they are not even for hindering or forwarding certain actions. They are simply calculated to check corruption in the great masses, to destroy, without mercy, what can no more be restored, and with new powers to give birth to new creations. Wherefore He does signs and wonders that interrupt and shake the course of things, and sends ambassadors, with more or less of divine spirit indwelling, to pour out divine powers among men.

And when man does seek through self-consciousness to enter into fellowship with the unity of the Whole, the finite resists him, and he seeks and does not find and loses what he has found. He is defective, variable and attached to details and non-essentials. He wills rather than gives heed, and his aim vanishes from his eyes. In vain is every revelation. Everything is swallowed up by the earthly sense, everything is swept away by the innate irreligious principle. The Deity finds ever new devices. By His power alone, ever more glorious revelations issue from the bosom of the old. He sets up ever more exalted mediators between Himself and men. In every later ambassador the Deity unites with humanity ever more closely, that men may learn to know the Eternal Being. Yet the ancient complaint that man cannot comprehend what is from the Spirit of God is never taken away.

This is how Christianity most and best is conscious of God, and of the divine order in religion and history. It manipulates religion itself as matter for religion. It is thus a higher power of religion, and this most distinguishes its character and determines its whole form. Because it presupposes a widely-extended godlessness it is through and through polemical. It is polemical in its outward communication, for, to make its deepest nature evident, every corruption must be laid bare, be it in morals or in thinking. Above all it must expose the hostility to the consciousness of the Highest Being, which is the irreligious principle itself. Relentlessly it unmasks every false morality, every bad religion, every unhappy union of both for mutual covering of nakedness. Into the inmost secrets of the corrupt heart it presses and illumines, with the sacred torch of personal experience, every evil that creeps in darkness. Almost its first work on appearing was to destroy the last expectation of its pious contemporaries, saying it was irreligious and godless to expect any other restoration than restoration to purer faiths, to the higher view of things and to eternal life in God. Boldly it led the heathen beyond the separation they had made between the world of the gods and the world of men. Not to live and move and have the being in God is to be entirely ignorant of Him. If this natural feeling, this inner consciousness is lost amid a mass of sense impressions and desires, no religion has yet entered the narrow sense. Everywhere, then, its heralds tore open the whited sepulchres and brought the dead bones to light. Had these first heroes of Christianity been philosophers, they would have spoken as strongly against the corruption of philosophy. They never failed to recognize the outlines of the divine image. Behind all distortions and degradations they saw hidden the heavenly germ of religion. But as Christians they were chiefly concerned with the individual who was far from God and needed a mediator.

Christianity, moreover, is as sharply and strongly polemical within its own borders, and in the inmost fellowship of the saints. Just because religion is nowhere so fully idealized as in Christianity, through its original postulate, perpetual warfare against all that is actual in religion is presented as a duty that can never be sufficiently fulfilled. And just because the ungodly is everywhere operative, because all actuality together appears unholy, an infinite holiness is the aim of Christianity. Never content with its attainments, it seeks, even in its purest productions, even in its holiest feelings, traces of irreligion and of the tendency of all finite things to turn away from the unity of the Whole. In the tone of the highest inspiration an ancient writer criticizes the religious state of the community; in simple openness the great apostles speak of themselves. And this is how every man is to walk in the sacred circle. He is not only to be an inspired man and a teacher, but in humility he is to present himself also to the universal testing. Nor shall anything be spared, not even what is most loved and dear; nor shall anything be indolently put aside, not even what is most generally acknowledged. Though without it be praised as holy and be set up before the world as the essence of religion, within it must be subjected to a severe and repeated test. Thus impurities are to be removed, and the splendor of the heavenly colors to shine more clearly in every pious impulse of the spirit.

In nature you often see a compound mass, as soon as its chemical powers have overcome outside resistance or reduced it to equilibrium, take to fermenting, and eject one and another element. So it is with Christianity, it turns at last its polemical power against itself. Ever anxious, lest in its struggle with external irreligion it has admitted something alien, or may yet have in itself some principle of corruption, it does not avoid even the fiercest inward commotions to eject the evil.

This is the history of Christianity that is rooted in its very nature. "I am not come to bring peace, but a sword," the Founder Himself said. His gentle soul could not possibly have meant that He was come to occasion those bloody commotions, so utterly contrary to the spirit of religion, or that wretched strife of words that deals with dead matter which living religion does not admit. But what He did foresee, and in foreseeing command, were those holy wars that spring necessarily from the essence of His teaching, and which, as bitterly as He describes, rend hearts asunder and dissolve the most intimate relations of life.

But not only are the elements of Christianity themselves subjected to this perpetual sifting; in their unbroken existence and life in the spirit there is an insatiable longing for ever stricter purification, ever richer fullness. Irreligion is thought to dominate every moment in which the religious principle is not evident in the mind. Religion has no other opposite than just the absence of religious purpose: every interruption of religion is irreligion. If the mind is for a moment without intuition and feeling of the Infinite, it at once becomes conscious of hostility and remoteness. Christianity then demands as first and essential that piety be a constant state. It scorns to be satisfied, even with the strongest displays of it, as soon as it only rules certain portions of the life. Piety should never rest, and there should never be anything so absolutely opposed as to be inconsistent with it. From all finite things we should see the Infinite. We should be in a position to associate religious feelings and views with all sentiments, however they may have arisen, and with all actions, whatever be their object. That is the true highest aim of mastery in Christianity.

How the fundamental view in Christianity, the view to which all others are referred, determines the character of its feelings is easy to discover. What do you call that feeling of an unsatisfied longing which is directed towards a great object, and which you are conscious is infinite? What impresses you on finding the sacred and the profane, the noble with the common and the mean intimately united? And what is the mood that urges you at times to assume the universality of this combination, and to search for it everywhere? With Christians this holy sadness is not occasional, but is the dominant tone of all their religious feelings. That is the only name which the language affords me. It accompanies every joy and every pain, every love and every fear. Nay, in its pride and in its humility it is the ground tone. If you can reconstruct the depths of a spirit from single features, undisturbed by foreign elements that have come from who knows where, you will find this feeling throughout dominant in the Founder of Christianity. If a writer, who has left but a few leaves in a simple speech is not too unimportant for your attention, you will discover this tone in every word remaining to us from his bosom friend. And if ever a Christian has allowed you to listen in the sanctuary of his soul, you have certainly caught just the same tone.

Such is Christianity. Its distortions and manifold corruptions I will not spare, for the corruptibility of every holy thing, as soon as it becomes human, is part of its fundamental view of the world. And I will

not go farther into the details of it. Its doings are
before you, and I believe I have given you the thread
that, guiding you through all anomalies, will make
the closest scrutiny possible. From first to last look
only at the clearness, the variety, and the richness
with which that first idea has been developed.

When, in the mutilated delineations of His life
I contemplate the sacred image of Him who has been
the author of the noblest that there has yet been in
religion, it is not the purity of His moral teaching,
which but expressed what all men who have come to
consciousness of their spiritual nature, have with Him
in common, and which, neither from its expression nor
its beginning, can have greater value, that I admire;
and it is not the individuality of His character, the
close union of high power with touching gentleness,
for every noble, simple spirit must in a special situation
display some traces of a great character. All those
things are merely human. But the truly divine element
is the glorious clearness to which the great idea He
came to exhibit attained in His soul. This idea was,
that all that is finite requires a higher mediation to be
in accord with the Deity, and that for man under the
power of the finite and particular, and too ready to
imagine the divine itself in this form, salvation is only
to be found in redemption. Vain folly it is to wish to
remove the veil that hides the rise of this idea in
Him, for every beginning in religion, as elsewhere,
is mysterious. The prying sacrilege that has attempted
it can only distort the divine. He is supposed to have
taken His departure from the ancient idea of His
people, and He only wished to utter its abolition
which, by declaring Himself to be the Person they

expected, He did most gloriously accomplish. Let us consider the living sympathy for the spiritual world that filled His soul, simply as we find it complete in Him.

If all finite things require the mediation of a higher being, if it is not to be ever further removed from the Eternal and be dispersed into the void and transitory, if its union with the Whole is to be sustained and come to consciousness, what mediates must not again require mediation, and cannot be purely finite. It must belong to both sides, participating in the Divine Essence in the same way and in the same sense in which it participates in human nature. But what did He see around Him that was not finite and in need of mediation, and where was aught that could mediate but Himself? "No man knoweth the Father but the Son, and He to whom the Son shall reveal Him." This consciousness of the singularity of His knowledge of God and of His existence in God, of the original way in which this knowledge was in Him, and of the power thereof to communicate itself and awake religion, was at once the consciousness of His office as mediator and of His divinity.

I would not speak of Him as standing opposed to the rude power of His foes without hope of longer life, for that is unspeakably unimportant. But when, forsaken in the thought of being silenced for ever, without seeing any outward institution for fellowship among His own actually set up, when in the face of the solemn splendor of the old corrupt system that had so mightily resisted Him, when surrounded by all that could inspire awe and demand subjection, by all that, from childhood, He had been taught to honor, sustained by nothing but that feeling, He uttered without delay that Yea, the greatest word mortal ever spake, it was the most glorious apotheosis, and no divinity can be more certain than that which He Himself thus proclaimed.

With this faith in Himself, who can wonder at His assurance that He was not only a mediator for many, but would leave behind a great school that would derive their religion from His? So certain was He that before it yet existed He appointed symbols for it. This He did in the conviction that they would suffice to bring the band of His disciples to a secure existence. Nay, so sure was He that already He had spoken among His own, with prophetic enthusiasm, of the immortalization of His memory.

Yet He never maintained He was the only mediator, the only one in whom His idea actualized itself. All who attach themselves to Him and form His church should also be mediators with Him and through Him. And He never made His school equivalent to His religion, as if His idea were to be accepted on account of His person, and not His person on account of His idea. Nay, He would even suffer His mediatorship to be undecided, if only the spirit, the principle from which His religion developed in Himself and others were not blasphemed.

His disciples also were far from confusing this school with His religion. Pupils of the Baptist, still only very imperfectly initiated into the nature of Christianity, were, without anything further, regarded and treated by the apostles as Christians and reckoned genuine members of the community. And it should be so still. Everyone who, in his religion, sets out from the same cardinal point, whether his religion originates from himself or from another, is, without respect of school, a Christian. It will naturally follow that when Christ with His whole efficacy is shown him he must acknowledge Him, who has become historically the center of all mediation, the true Founder of redemption and reconciliation.

Nor did Christ say that the religious views and feelings He Himself could communicate, were the whole extent of the religion that should proceed from this ground-feeling. He always pointed to the living truth which, though only "taking of His," would come after Him. Similarly with His disciples. They never set limits to the Holy Spirit. His unbounded freedom and the absolute unity of His revelations are everywhere acknowledged by them.

And when, the first bloom of Christianity being past and it was appearing to rest from its works, those works, so far as they were contained in the sacred scriptures, were regarded as a finished codex of religion, it was only brought about by those who took the slumber of the Spirit for death—religion, as far as they were concerned, being dead. All who still feel the life of religion in themselves or perceive it in others, have ever protested against this unchristian proceeding. The sacred scriptures have, by their native power, become a bible, and forbid no other book to be or to become a bible. Anything written with like power they would willingly allow to be associated with themselves. Nay, should not every later utterance of the whole church, and therefore of the Divine Spirit, append itself confidently, even though there be ineffaceably in the first fruits of the Spirit a special holiness and worth?

In accordance with this unlimited freedom, this essential infinity, then, this leading idea of Christianity of divine mediating powers has in many ways been developed, and all intuitions and feelings of the indwelling of the Divine Being in finite nature have within Christianity been brought to perfection. Thus very soon Holy Scripture in which, in its own way, divine essence and heavenly power dwelt, was held as a logical mediator to open for the knowledge of God the finite and corrupt nature of the understanding, while the Holy Spirit, in a later acceptation of the word, was an ethical mediator, whereby to draw near to the Deity in action. Nay, a numerous party of Christians declare themselves ready to acknowledge everyone as a mediating and divine being who can prove, by a divine life or any impress of divineness, that he has been, for even a small circle, the first quickening of the higher sense. To others Christ has remained one and all, while others have declared that their mediators have been their own selves or some particular thing. Whatever failure there may have been in form and matter, the principle is genuinely Christian, so long as it is free. Other human situations have, in their relation to the central point of Christianity, been expressed by feelings and represented by images, of which there is no hint in the speeches of Christ or elsewhere in the sacred books. Hereafter there will be more, for the whole being of man is not yet by any means embodied in the peculiar form of Christianity, but, despite what is said of its speedy, its already accomplished overthrow, Christianity will yet have a long history.

For why should it be overthrown? The living

spirit of it, indeed, slumbers oft and long. It withdraws itself into a torpid state, into the dead shell of
the letter, but it ever awakes again as soon as the
season in the spiritual world is favorable for its re-
vival and sets its sap into motion. Thus in oft repeated
cycle it renews itself in various ways. The fundamental idea of every positive religion, being a component part of the infinite Whole in which all things
must be eternal, is itself eternal and universal, but
its whole development, its temporal existence may
not, in the same sense, be either universal or eternal.
For to put the center of religion just in that idea, it
requires not only a certain mental attitude, but a certain state of mankind. Is this state, in the free play
of the universal life, gone, never to return, that relation which, by its worth, made all others dependent
on it, can no longer maintain itself in the feeling, and
this type of religion can no more endure. This is the
case with all childlike religions, as soon as men lose
the consciousness of their essential power. They should
be collected as monuments of the past and deposited
in the magazine of history, for their life is gone, never
to return. Christianity, exalted above them all, more
historical and more humble in its glory, has expressly
acknowledged this transitoriness of its temporal existence. A time will come, it says, when there shall
no more be any mediator, but the Father shall be all
in all. But when shall this time come? I, at least, can
only believe that it lies beyond all time.

One half of the original intuition of Christianity
is the corruptibleness of all that is great and divine
in human things. If a time should come when this—
I will not say can no more be discovered, but no more

obtrudes, when humanity advances so uniformly and peacefully, that only the navigator who calculates its course by the stars knows when it is somewhat driven back on the great ocean it traverses by a passing contrary wind, and the unarmed eye, looking only at what is taking place, can no more directly observe the retrogression of human affairs, I would gladly stand on the ruins of the religion I honor.

The other half of the original Christian faith is that certain brilliant and divine points are the source of every improvement in this corruption and of every new and closer union of the finite with the Deity. Should a time ever come, when the power that draws us to the Highest was so equally distributed among the great body of mankind, that persons more strongly moved should cease to mediate for others, I would fain see it, I would willingly help to level all that exalteth itself. But this equality of all equalities is least possible. Times of corruption await all human things, even though of divine origin. New ambassadors from God will be required with exalted power to draw the recreant to itself and purify the corrupt with heavenly fire, and every such epoch of humanity is a palingenesis of Christianity, and awakes its spirit in a new and more beautiful form.

And if there are always to be Christians, is Christianity, therefore, to be universal and, as the sole type of religion, to rule alone in humanity? It scorns this autocracy. Every one of its elements it honors enough to be willing to see it the center of a whole of its own. Not only would it produce in itself variety to infinity, but would willingly see even outside all that it cannot produce from itself. Never forgetting that it has the best proof of its immortality in its own corruptibleness, in its own often sad history, and ever expecting a redemption from the imperfection that now oppresses it, it willingly sees other and younger, and, if possible, stronger and more beautiful types of religion arise outside of this corruption. It could see them arise close beside it, and issue from all points even from such as appear to it the utmost and most doubtful limits of religion. The religion of religions cannot collect material enough for its pure interest in all things human. As nothing is more irreligious than to demand general uniformity in mankind, so nothing is more unchristian than to seek uniformity in religion.

In all ways the Deity is to be contemplated and worshiped. Varied types of religion are possible, both in proximity and in combination, and if it is necessary that every type be actualized at one time or another, it is to be desired that, at all times, there should be a dim sense of many religions. The great moments must be few in which all things agree to ensure to one among them a wide-extended and enduring life, in which the same view is developed unanimously and irresistibly in a great body, and many persons are deeply affected by the same impression of the divine. Yet what may not be looked for from a time that is so manifestly the border land between two different orders of things? If only the intense crisis were past, such a moment might arrive. Even now a prophetic soul, such as the fiery spirits of our time have, turning its thought to creative genius, might perhaps indicate the point that is to be for the future generations the center for their fellowship with the Deity. But how-

ever it be, and however long such a moment may still
linger, new developments of religion, whether under
Christianity or alongside of it, must come and that
soon, even though for a long time they are only
discernible in isolated and fleeting manifestations. Out
of nothing a new creation always comes forth, and in
all living men in whom the intellectual life has power
and fullness, religion is almost nothing. From some
one of the countless occasions it will be developed in
many and take new shape in new ground. Were but
the time of caution and timidity past! Religion hates
loneliness, and in youth especially, which for all things
is the time of love, it wastes away in a consuming
longing. When it is developed in you, when you are
conscious of the first traces of its life, enter at once
into the one indivisible fellowship of the saints, which
embraces all religions and in which alone any can
prosper. Do you think that because the saints are
scattered and far apart, you must speak to unsanctified
ears? You ask what language is secret enough—is it
speech, writing, deed, or quiet copying of the Spirit?
All ways, I answer, and you see that I have not
shunned the loudest. In them all sacred things remain
secret and hidden from the profane. They may gnaw
at the shell as they are able, but to worship the God
that is in you, do you not refuse us.